D0508044

WALKING WITH THE ANGELS

Some further books of White Eagle's teaching:

BEAUTIFUL ROAD HOME

THE BOOK OF STAR LIGHT

THE GENTLE BROTHER

GOLDEN HARVEST

HEAL THYSELF

JESUS TEACHER AND HEALER

THE LIVING WORD OF ST JOHN

MORNING LIGHT

THE PATH OF THE SOUL

PRAYER IN THE NEW AGE

THE QUIET MIND

THE SOURCE OF ALL OUR STRENGTH

SPIRITUAL UNFOLDMENT 1

SPIRITUAL UNFOLDMENT 2

SPIRITUAL UNFOLDMENT 3

SPIRITUAL UNFOLDMENT 4

THE STILL VOICE

SUNRISE

THE WAY OF THE SUN

WISDOM FROM WHITE EAGLE

Boxed sets of Affirmation Cards

FACE THE SUN

WINGS OF LIGHT

Walking with the Angels

A PATH OF SERVICE

White Eagle
Additional commentary by Anna Hayward

THE WHITE EAGLE PUBLISHING TRUST
NEW LANDS · LISS · HAMPSHIRE · ENGLAND

First published November 1998
Reprinted July 2000
© The White Eagle Publishing Trust, 1998
Calligraphy © Gaynor Goffe, 1998

British Library Cataloguing-in-Publication Data
A catalogue record for this book is
available from the British Library

ISBN 0-85487-109-8

Set in 11 & 12 on 15 pt Baskerville by
the publisher, and printed and bound in Great Britain
at the University Press, Cambridge

CONTENTS

FOREWORD

One of the significant qualities of White Eagle's teaching is that in it he has the ability to appear to us both as 'the gentle brother' and as the great mystic. In this book we find the two aspects of White Eagle represented. The first is demonstrated by his love and concern for the struggles of our human existence and the advice he gives as to how we can best deal with them from a spiritual perspective. The second is shown by the glimpse he gives us of how, even from his viewpoint, the cosmic plan for humanity and angels is both magnificent and awesome.

For this reason, many passages of White Eagle's teaching in this book are both poetic and mystical. Through this he manages to convey something of the mystery of spiritual life, and to prevent us from cataloguing and rationalizing profound truths with the earthly mind in a way which would give us a restrictive and only partial understanding. White Eagle asks us to read with what he calls the 'mind in the heart': from that place within us all which is knowledgable beyond the limitations of the ordinary mind, and which responds to the beauty and poetry of life. This may indeed be the very part of us all which is closest to the angels.

As the title suggests, WALKING WITH THE ANGELS is a book of White Eagle's teaching about the angels and their work. It is also a guide to the best way we may learn to work with them. In order to create the most harmonious conditions within ourselves that allow us to become more aware of the angelic presence all about us, it is helpful to examine what quality of motivation is needed.

The major part of the book consists of previously unpublished teaching by White Eagle, plus a few passages from earlier books, but there is also commentary which, it is hoped, will help readers in becoming more aware of the angels and in developing those qualities in themselves to which the angels are most attuned. The title also points to one very clear aspect of our relationship with the angels and their work, namely our common service to humanity and all life.

Because the book has this emphasis on the importance of our motivation and attunement, it is divided into two parts; and the first of these is given over to the qualities we may wish to develop in ourselves in order to contact and work with the angels in their service. Immediately after Part One, I have included the White Eagle Prayer for Humanity, as an example of how we can act in harmony with the angels to give service to humanity.

In Part Two White Eagle describes the immense and magnificent structure of the angelic stream, and its different forms. More of his teaching about the angels and the elemental kingdoms can be found in the books SPIRITUAL UNFOLDMENT II and SUN-MEN OF THE AMERICAS.*

For some, it may take a degree of courage to acknowledge an interest and belief in angels. Many people see stories about them as only mythology. Yet White Eagle says that without angelic influence humanity would actually cease to exist, for the angels are intimately connected with all creation. Moreover, those people who do seek an understanding of the angelic stream of life may themselves resonate, in some way, with the creative impulse: not only in the arts, but through their whole response to life. People who believe in angels are content neither to let material life dictate to them, nor to follow only the evidence of the narrow physical senses. Rather, they live their lives in appreciation of a greater beauty, wisdom and love. They sense that there is something lovelier and more powerful than we can conceive, beyond and behind all physical manifestations. Such people are often seeking a meaning in life as well as ways to alleviate suffer-

*White Eagle Publishing Trust, 1969, 1975

ing and create more beauty. Those who seek balance and wish to create harmonious conditions for all are responding, perhaps unconsciously, to the angels.

Since the angels are so deeply connected with the creation of form in all its manifestations, anyone who seeks to bring entirely new conceptions into life does so through their help. Moreover, if it is in one's heart to respond creatively and appropriately to all the conditions of life, if one wishes to learn and to become more aware, and if, furthermore, there is a wish to flow with the divine plan and respond to that plan as best one can, then the angels are able to bring inspiration and guidance. For all that, we must not think that it is only when we become perfectly receptive and pure in motive that they draw close, for they are always there beside us. When we sincerely open ourselves to serve divine love in all its aspects, then they are able to use that aspiration and commitment.

Often it is in small ways that we suddenly find ourselves in the angels' presence. When we let go of the limitations and the fears which rule the instinctive mind, body and emotions; when with the innocence of a child we approach the beauty and harmony of our natural world and the spiritual spheres, then these beings of pure love and service respond. A sudden feeling of exquisite joy and tenderness as we gaze at a newborn baby or animal; a vision of sweeping light in the branches of a tree tossed by the wind; a sensation of oneness and immensity under the blazing stars; the realization of the perfection of the tiniest flower; a deep sense of connection as we walk over the earth and the grass; an appreciation of sound so lovely it almost hurts: who is to say that in these moments we are not experiencing an angelic contact? We need no special gifts; this realm is open to us all.

What I hope that White Eagle's teaching on angels will do for the reader is to bring reassurance that life indeed has a far greater meaning and purpose than we know. Perhaps, for the reader as for me, his words will unlock an inner door—a portal through which we can see reality not merely as hardship and illusion, but full of creative possibilities and wonder. It is my belief that through contact with the angelic life, if only through reading, we can find ourselves knowing, more and more, just how deeply we are loved, and by what power, wisdom and compassion our lives are guided and sustained.

Anna Hayward

Publisher's note

Free reference is made to other White Eagle books in print, a list of which is given opposite the title page. All are published by the White Eagle Publishing Trust.

White Eagle's own words are indented and in larger type; the commentary is shown in the smaller type. Biblical quotations and poetry are in italics.

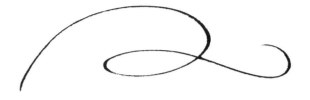

PART ONE

1. Introduction to Part One: the Angelic Qualities

White Eagle's opening words introduce one of the central principles of his teaching, the presence within us all of a true Christ light, a spiritual light. From this, he says, all understanding flows.

The starting point for all investigation into the unknown must be from one humble and simple truth—the Christ light within yourself. Let us think of ourselves, as did the ancients, as comprising a universe within, as being ourselves a microcosm. We must realize that we are related to every manifestation of God, both upon earth and in the heavens. Whatever lies in the heavens above, what seems infinitely removed, is actually also within ourselves. We are in affinity with all planes of life, from the lowest to the highest. Within ourselves—physical, etheric, mental and spiritual—are the identical life-atoms to be found in spheres far from the earth. More than this, there is within each soul a correlation with the planets and with the influences and even the ethers of the planets. And thus we are linked with the planetary angels, and all the angelic hierarchy, while on the evolutionary path.

Please do not limit your conception of the invisible worlds which surround the earth. These commence with the planes of ether within the earth itself and rise to the highest that it is possible for humanity to reach. Also, even if we, or any other teacher, talk to you about the different planes and the different spheres of life, remember they are interpenetrating and inseparable—life is one whole.

One of the purposes of this book is to demonstrate just how impossible it is to be separate from the rest of the universe, from God, or from the angels. The angelic stream of evolution is intimately connected with our own. Furthermore, this oneness of life means that our contact with the angels begins not in escaping from the earth plane, but in becoming increasingly aware within our own being. This is not an absorption with the self so much as a looking beneath the surface of life to the true heart of the self which is connected with God. Being connected with God we are linked with every other person, animal and life-form on the planet; and beyond this to the stars themselves, and to the spiritual dimensions which interpenetrate it all. 'What seems infinitely removed, is actually also within ourselves.' White Eagle places great emphasis on our developing an awareness of this inter–connectedness of all life, for it is the recognition of this which enables us truly to understand the value of life, service to others, and the preservation of beauty and harmony throughout the whole world—in effect, to understand a little of the divine purpose which the angels serve.

In the following passage, part of which was printed in a slightly reduced version in SPIRITUAL UNFOLDMENT II, White Eagle gives us a vision:

You look up at the sky at night and you see countless millions of lights—you call them stars—and you think you are looking upon a vast universe, but you know nothing of the life which is living, moving and having its being within that universe. Your physical eye cannot see, nor your physical brain comprehend, the vastness of that invisible universe. And yet, if you are learning to enter the stillness within your simple heart, you can begin to understand a little more of what lies in that visible and invisible universe. If you can feel the heartbeat of sympathy, you begin to feel harmony, to see vibrations in the form of colour. You become aware of other creatures, apart from humanity; apart from the animal world and the vegetable world.

Walk into your garden and be still, withdraw into the temple of silence. If only for a flash, you may become aware of the numberless creatures: the nature spirits, fairies, gnomes; even the very stones are inhabited by etheric folk.* Yet in the ordinary way all you see is the outer form of your pretty flowers. If you stop to think, you will wonder how the flowers are brought into blossom, what brings their perfume, what it is that makes one flower yellow, another pink, and the leaves green. What power lies behind?

Make no mistake! The human race, whether it knows it or not, lives through all time under the guardianship of God's

---

*Readers from some cultural or religious backgrounds may find it easier to accept White Eagle's teaching on angels and their wide service to all life than the idea of 'nature spirits, fairies, gnomes'. However, White Eagle has always talked of a whole spectrum of invisible life, with energies ranging from the playful, small and light to the infinitely majestic. A short personal story contributed by my husband Jeremy may illustrate this:

'Once when gathering vegetables from the organic garden at the White Eagle Lodge I found myself using one of White Eagle's Native American prayers to say 'thank you' for the leaves and roots I was gathering. I most distinctly felt an answering impulse of joy, as if voices were saying 'Yes, that's us! That's us!' In all that playful light response—their pleasure at being recognized— I knew that I had touched the consciousness of those whom White Eagle variously calls 'fairies' or 'etheric workers' (p. 16). This aspect of the angelic life is every bit as real and accessible as the grander aspects depicted in this book; it is more specifically described in White Eagle's book SPIRITUAL UNFOLDMENT II.

angels. Humanity has always walked the earth with angels. The angels come through a different line of evolution from that followed by human kind, although it is parallel to the human line, and the angels are closely linked with humanity and help you with your work and life on earth.

A certain line of angelic creation is concerned purely with the soul of things, with the attributes both of the soul of a human being and the soul of the universe. Divine attributes such as love are served by the angels of love; divine truth by the angels of truth, divine mercy by the angels of mercy. So the angels have to do with the soul of things, and make manifest the attributes of the soul. For example, the angels of music are concerned with the creation of the form and sound of music in order to bring forth, from silence, sound. They produce music to enable the body and spirit to hear the divine harmonies. The angels of art are concerned with the vibrations of colour; the angels of religion assist in the creation, or building up of spiritual power in worship of the divine. There is also the dual aspect of the angelic kingdom: the angels of the light and of the dark. These two aspects work together to bring about balance—one of the fundamental laws of life.

As we have said, the way to know all these things is to find God within; to know God within one's heart. And until a person does know God he or she cannot gain any understanding of the universe. It is from the Christ, both within and in the heavens, that you must commence to learn all these glorious truths. The angels, and the heavenly spheres from which they descend to your level, are not as remote as you may think: heaven is within, and you must learn to find heaven within while you are still in a physical body.

When White Eagle talks about learning to 'find heaven within', while still in a physical body, in order to understand and contact the angelic realm, what does he mean? Angels, he says, 'have to do with the soul of things, and make manifest the attributes of the soul'. Therefore he encourages us to develop the soul qualities of which the angels are composed in order to contact them. For example, to contact the angels of peace, one has to develop peace within oneself. One can only contact and be aware of the angels through the development of the vibrations within oneself which will be in harmony with theirs. We cannot expect to see angels when we go into the woods and fields, or visit the sacred places of our lands, unless we are resonating to their vibration. This may sound difficult, but our aspiration and our openness, our belief in the interconnectedness of our life and theirs, are the keys.

This may simply mean that we ask for their help, for example, in becoming more peaceful and still. That help will surely come if we are truly prepared to *be* peaceful, and willing to let go of that in us which is getting in the way of peace and stillness. Then the angels of peace are able to draw close to help us develop this soul quality, because this is one of their tasks.

Besides showing us how to resonate in harmony with the angelic vibration through this soul development, White Eagle talks about the importance of how we are thinking: the need for purity of thought and for positive thought in our approach to life.

We often refer to the presence of angels, but perhaps you do not realize yet the importance of the angelic work? We wish you to understand that it is the combination of the nature forces with human thought-power which causes certain manifestation in human life on the physical plane. Humanity cannot work alone; you must know how to call upon the nature forces whose work it is to assist a person of the light in his or her work. Thus it is as well for you to understand the importance of your daily thought, of your daily attitude of mind towards everyday life and the simple things. The deeper you probe into the spiritual mysteries of life the more important becomes purity of thought and aspiration. But thought in itself can be of little power unless animated by the spirit.

The old philosophers used to say, 'As above, so below'. As you see in your meditations, and as you learn to meditate wisely, purely and truly, you will bring through into manifestation on earth what you see shining above in that state of meditation. You are God's instruments on earth. You can give a great deal of help to the etheric workers, to those who work with the growing plants for humanity's sustenance; to the angels of the air who inspire humanity in the creative arts and in all works of creation, and most of all you can help by your God-thought and by your love. All good thoughts which you have for your earthly companions reach their mark. They register as light. From the body of light thus built up, the angels work to carry good thought to others, so that still more souls in incarnation receive these currents of constructive thought. There is then built up a very great power of good thought, of light.

This reservoir of power and love you build with the help of the angels of form. It is their work to take and make into form the thoughts and aspirations which flow from your higher selves.

Thus it is that the angels draw close to all who pray sincerely for peace, healing, love and beauty, for their loved ones, humanity, and for the earth itself.

Attunement to the Angelic Presence

> Men and women will walk and talk with angels, but remember, it takes an angel to recognize an angel. You attract to yourself that which you are yourself; and so you need to develop the necessary qualities within yourself.

During the next few chapters we will be looking at White Eagle's description of the qualities associated with the angels, and the ways in which we can develop the answering qualities within ourselves. Eventually, if we are persevering and patient, it is possible so to attune ourselves to the angelic realm that we will be able to experience the angels' presence and work more closely with them. Through doing this we are seeking, as White Eagle says, to 'animate our thoughts with the power of the spirit'.

White Eagle has given a description of the angels' etheric appearance. Though you may not be able, at present, to 'see' these beings, White Eagle's vision of their form (or at least how they might appear to us) helps to give a feeling of the angels' presence. This feeling, along with some understanding of their nature, which is conveyed in what follows, builds an impression in the mind and heart of each of us. This impression, encouraged by contemplation and meditation, becomes a vibration to which the angels are drawn.

> The angels who guard and love you from the spirit world are very joyous at your response to their influence and their help. It would not do for you to have your eyes fully opened to the radiance of the spiritual beings who work with you—you could not stand to live in your earthly life if you felt too powerfully the vibrations of these Godlike brethren. But we would convey to you occasionally a picture of their beauty and love. You talk of love and aspire to love; you do

so valiantly in your service, but even so, you cannot yet comprehend the beauty of these angelic ministers.

The angels are beings twice and thrice your own stat-
ure, beings with great wings and auras radiant and limit-
less. Great rays of light pour from them like feathery plumes,
like white wings, and they bring you peace and love. The
emanation from them, coming in circles from the head, gives
the appearance of wings. When we speak of winged beings
you will understand that the emanation coming from these
etheric beings takes the form of wings, so that looking at
them fleetingly you would get the impression of tall human
forms with wings. These 'wings' are rays of power and
strength; they can be enfolding and protecting, and from
them emanate God-forces.

2. The Angelic Quality of Dispassion

White Eagle once said,

> Will you try to understand the love which the angels bring?
> Angels are supposed to be quite impersonal; this may be so
> according to earthly standards of feelings and emotion, but
> the angels' love is pure and utterly selfless.

Reinforcing this, in A WHITE EAGLE LODGE BOOK OF HEALTH AND HEAL-
ING,* Joan Hodgson writes: 'Perhaps the greatest difference between
the human line of evolution and the angelic is that humans feel emotion whereas the angels work with absolute dispassion in obedience
to a divine plan, an infinitely beautiful cosmic design. The guardian
angel in charge of each human life holds that life under a ray of light
and power which ensures the completion of the design for a particular incarnation. One might almost liken the working of the angelic
kingdom to a cosmic computer under the control of the divine mind'.

It is important to retain an awareness of the angels' dispassion.
One cannot contact the angels with a heart full of emotionalism of
any kind, since their love is one based on knowledge and awareness
of the justice and wisdom of the divine—an awareness of the whole

*White Eagle Publishing Trust, 1983, p. 180

of life—which means they see the true need of the soul, and the true need of humanity of which the individual soul is a part. They act spontaneously from love, but from a love which is divine and linked with wisdom and power: a love which goes beyond the personal.

One might say that their love is inextricably linked with the oneness of all life, and serves that wholeness. It is not limited to the individual and, being utterly selfless, it can only serve the karma and dharma of all. Even the guardian angel, who is with each one from before their birth, will be serving more than the present-day personality. The angels bring a feeling of the most profound kind of love, one which, far from stirring up the emotions, actually enables us to gain a measure of detachment and equanimity. Through this balanced, wise love we are able to see our karma and dharma (that is, our challenges and the opportunities they bring) from a more helpful perspective, so that we can perhaps handle them better.

Again White Eagle says:

The angels are not disturbed by *any* world problem, for they know only one truth: that all is working together for good. They come to help humanity realize this one grand truth ... *all is working together for good*. If you would understand them, you must yield yourself and become obedient to the divine within, saying: 'thy will be done; thou art the Creator; thou art creating thy child, thy son—daughter; we bow in thankfulness, and have no fear'. Get above fear thought; get beyond and above, and live in the positive thought of good becoming manifest on all planes of being.

It is not only world problems which disturb us. White Eagle knows how much our equanimity is thrown by concerns for our loved ones. He has the following to say about the kind of love to develop for those close to us, the brothers and sisters of our spirit, so that it is freeing and constructive.

> God knows the need of the soul for companionship. God created human beings to be companions and brothers and lovers to each other. But, in order not to be enslaved by the earthly personality, you need to develop dispassion. One way to do this is to centre your whole being and aspiration upon God and try to see, through all your personal relationships, the great Being. Try to see in your brother, father, husband, an expression (however small it may appear) of the divine Father. Try to recognize in womankind the divine Mother. Both principles have to be developed in every soul. If you can realize this truth it will help you to overcome the stumbling block of personality. Within, you will be free.

There are various occasions when we can learn to develop dispassion, and thus be more in harmony with the deeper constructive forces of the spirit and the angels which manipulate them. Dispassion may be needed in our own feelings about making contact with angels. The same thing is true of meditation, in that if we want the experience with too much desire, too much of the self, then that contact is elusive. Paradoxically, we still need to persevere and to retain the aspiration. The Taoists have an expression for the juxtaposition of these two attitudes. They call it 'wu wei'—'effortless effort'. White Eagle calls it 'desirelessness'.

To be too ardent in our desires to succeed or to attain something, even contact with the angels, produces passion and high excitement rather than dispassion. It makes us overly emotional in the face of seeming failure and success. It produces a strong attachment to what *we* want, and this may not be the same as the need of the soul. It can result in us becoming very self-absorbed. Joan Hodgson, this time in her book PLANETARY HARMONIES,* writes: 'Many people are so anxious to see into the inner world, so eager for psychic experience, that they palpitate with excitement, enthusiasm and maybe apprehension also. This state of mind closes the door firmly on the possibility of conscious contact. The outer mind is just too eager and too brash to be able to touch or comprehend this inner world, even though it is so close to the physical'.

And White Eagle says (in the book WISDOM FROM WHITE EAGLE):

As soon as people awaken and consciously tread the spiritual path, their desire is to know more and more. The soul becomes greedy, avid for knowledge, but this must be curbed. There must be self-discipline and development of tranquillity of soul. Tranquillity of soul is of utmost importance, because only in its tranquil moments is the soul receptive to the ministry of angels.

We are shown here the first step in developing equanimity—a poise of being, where we can open our hearts to the angels' presence—which is to let go our avidness for experience and knowledge. The foundation of a peaceful mind and emotions is trust. When we really trust in the great plan for all evolution, as the angels can, then we are swayed neither by sorrow nor by pleasure. We move through our life with our spine 'as a rod of light'. We can bend in humility and with compassion, but we can also stay balanced and strong in the light of the spirit.

This may seem like an impossible dream, but as in all spiritual things, our aspiration is what the angels respond to most. Our aura takes on the colours and vibrations of what is in our heart and heart-mind. The angels are etheric beings, and therefore intimately aware of the individual's aura. They sense the vibrations therein,

* White Eagle Publishing Trust, 1980, p. 24

and respond to them. Each aspiration to peace and equanimity, therefore, will be registered in the aura. Perhaps the individual may not be able to hold that state of balance for long, but still the angels sense the inner longing of the heart. They will then draw close to those who are seeking freedom from the agitation of the everyday mind and seeking to allow the deep peace of the inner self to arise and take control of their life.

What it may help to remember is that we all have that inner peace. It is not something vouchsafed to a few. No matter what kind of life we lead, nor whom we are with, there is within each one of us a place of tranquillity, not so far beneath the surface. Part of our trust in God is this faith in our own inner being. When White Eagle says elsewhere that God never leaves us without a 'witness', perhaps one of the things he is trying to convey is that we have been born, not wholly isolated in our body of flesh, but with an inner means of touching the spirit.

This, of course, does not mean that we cannot be joyous, happy, energetic and fun-loving, because these vibrations are also a part of love. They are creative of good, and angels draw close to all creativity of this kind in order to serve the development of humanity. However, lightness of heart and creative energy are different qualities from excitability. They come from an inner peace and poise, whereas excitability comes from an imbalance of energy and a tension which is disturbing to the nervous system and hence to the etheric body, through which the angels may otherwise make their presence known.

One of the qualities which balances desire and effort perfectly is humour. The ability to laugh at oneself, and to see the funny side of those situations when all our best-laid plans go awry, is invaluable to dispassion. Nothing ever seems quite so wrong, or so important, if one can see some humour in it. It is as if, at the moment the funny side of things touches you, much of the negativity of the situation is transformed: the smile and the laugh let the light in. You feel set free:

having been encased, seemingly, in a room with no exits, you find
that suddenly a window appears onto a garden, and the fresh air
streams in. And such is the way of things that, once the window has
appeared, then so does a door (humour being contagious), until the
lightened room is filled with possibilities for movement and colour. It
does not surprise me that the enlightened Buddha is always depicted
sitting with a wonderful smile on his face, nor that White Eagle often
talks about how he would like to see us smile more often.

The image of the Buddha is a good one to reflect upon when
thinking of developing dispassion. Here you have a figure that is
serene and noble; obviously beyond the passions of the world, yet
with that incredibly gentle smile. What thoughts can possibly be going through his mind, if thoughts there are? Maybe, that all is well;
all karma resolves itself; all is enfolded in the arms of God; that there
is nothing to fear; nothing, ultimately, to be sad for?

White Eagle gives us many descriptions to help us raise our awareness above the temptation to be anxious and sorrowful about our
karma and suffering. In his book HEAL THYSELF he says:

Every soul seems to suffer; but if you can see that suffering in
its right perspective you will see that it brings a rebirth.
Through limitation and suffering the soul emerges into the
divine life and light, just as the insect emerges from the
chrysalis stage into a beautiful winged creature in the sunlight.

To me the Buddha's whole posture brings the dispassionate yet
compassionate awareness to which White Eagle often refers. I have
before me an image from Thailand which particularly inspires me.
The Buddha's spine is erect, yet his base is firmly on the earth. His
whole being looks, in fact, like an upward-pointing triangle. His heart
area is completely open, and his hands lie on his lap in total trust and

receptivity. There is no sense of struggle or effort; no closing-in of the awareness and compassion out of fear; no passion or striving; but rather, complete openness to what is, what has been and what will be. He is centred in the moment, waiting patiently. He is still and at peace, yet you can feel the dynamic power and inner strength which that whole dispassion brings. His very dispassion and stillness create a vibration around him which attracts all-good; to which angels would be drawn.

So here we have two particular ways in which we can begin to free ourselves from the tyranny of desire, in its broadest sense: to tap into our sense of humour, and to contemplate and emulate the qualities and image of a master such as the Buddha. Both require a little more space than we may be accustomed to giving ourselves. By this I don't necessarily mean more meditation, but rather, creating space in everyday life, or space in the midst of activity, if we can. I mean deliberately making ourselves stop and *feel* inside; making ourselves really look around; making ourselves ponder carefully what is happening. Most of us tend to go from one thing to another and another, without true contemplation at all; we say things too quickly, agree to things too readily, make quick judgments of situations, and this partly because life seems to demand it. Yet at any moment—right this minute, or in the middle of typing, cooking, doing practically anything—for just a few moments we could stop and be more consciously aware either of our inner being, or of the world around. The Buddhists call it 'mindfulness'.

We can *always* give ourselves just a little more space to see and feel, and think with the deeper mind. When we do, remarkable things happen and all sorts of possibilities present themselves. There is then room for us to sense the ridiculous in a situation, or the loveliness, and perhaps to be aware of the different possibilities which the situation presents. There is the opportunity to detach from the onward rush of habitual thought, habitual feeling, and what one expects to see. In that space, other things become visible on all levels.

It is as if in those few moments you create a Buddha-stillness and receptivity. The moments don't have to last very long at all, but if you do this frequently, you will begin to notice a change in your awareness of daily life. The continual creation of moments of awareness and detachment will produce more dispassion. Being mindful will become a constant, rather than an intermittent way of being.

Besides this (I believe White Eagle would say), when you sit to meditate, and in your quiet times during the day, seek to sit as the Buddha does. Not necessarily in the lotus pose, or on the floor, but with the spine erect, the hands in the lap and the chest open and lifted, with the chin level. A picture of the Buddha like the one I described would help to give the idea. This very posture brings poise, a quality of dispassion. Allow your face to reflect the Buddhic smile, and imagine what it would be like to look upon life without fear, displeasure or desire, but with equanimity.

During the course of a meditation, White Eagle once gave this description of the contact which can be made with the angels in that attuned state, and the feeling which comes with their presence:

> Come with us into the heavenly garden and walk with the brethren of the light. Commune with the angelic company. Angels are unmoved by passion. They appear to be without emotion because they are emotionally still and disciplined. They live in the aura, the consciousness, the life of divine Mother, and in the infinite and eternal garden you will see angelic forces in colours unmatched on earth, still and peaceful, continually giving, giving, giving help; pouring love and wisdom upon creation.

3. A Natural and Joyous Path of Service

As we recognize the dispassion of the angelic kingdom, it deepens our awareness that in order to contact the angels our motives need to be based on something more than the surface desires of the personality. The dispassion of the angels is based on a love which goes beyond self-centredness so much that they respond constantly to the divine truth that all life is connected, that no one person can be separate or develop separately, and that as one person grows in God-consciousness and love, so do all.

The angels' work is the loving service of all creation, and therefore those who are consciously or unconsciously motivated in the same way automatically work with them. Some people make the conscious commitment to live out the angelic qualities in their own lives, not for themselves alone, but for the benefit of all. Others have such compassion and thoughtfulness for the world—for those who are suffering, for the animal kingdom, and for the earth herself—that they unconsciously attract the angels to them. And again, there are those who respond to the beauty of life and seek to share this, perhaps in creative work, so that others too find the angels' influence in their work.

Indeed, as can be seen from the following prayer, White Eagle says that the angels actually *call* us to service.

Be still, the mind of earth.... Let the higher mind open to the angelic forces. May your souls be bathed in the sunlight, in the golden light of the love, the power and the wisdom which is flowing from the heart of Christ. The angels call you to service; may your daily prayer be that you be made ready. The angels mingle with you and minister to all those who serve in the name of love.*

In another place, White Eagle has this to say:

The angels of light draw close to those who humbly and truly seek to serve the Great Spirit; and service, when selfless, when given freely and lovingly, is inspired by the angels of light working through the soul.
Angels of love, angels of wisdom, angels of power, these hosts will come to aid men and women as soon as ever humanity becomes humbled and trusting and loving towards them and their Master, the Christ.

The angels' very reason for being, therefore, is service. True service lies indeed in this acknowledgment of the interconnectedness of life. Once we become aware of how we are all linked together through the Christ love in our hearts, then an unselfconscious and natural longing to serve can come out of our empathy and deepest love.

The following story from the Tibetan tradition about the Buddha of Infinite Compassion, Avalokitesvara, demonstrates this. It is said that when he reached enlightenment Avalokitesvara was on his way to dwell in Nirvana when he looked back from above the earth at the suffering of humanity. In that instant he realized that he could

* One of the joys of reading the transcripts of White Eagle's talks is that he invariably began and ended the talk with a prayer such as this. Often during the prayer he would call on those listening to open their hearts to the presence of the angels, who would be present there.

not dwell in paradise while there were still people suffering on earth, and thus he stays within the aura of the earth to help humanity, each according to their need, until all beings are enlightened. Thus Avalokitesvara is depicted as having thousands of arms, with an all-seeing eye of wisdom in the palm of each hand. He is thus shown as helping each one in the wisest way, according to what they most need.*

The following are some lines from a poem, 'The Mistress of Vision', by the late nineteenth-century writer, Francis Thompson. They give another glimpse of this interconnectedness of all life, such that each individual's actions and reactions can affect the whole:

> *All things by immortal power,*
> *Near or far,*
> *Hiddenly*
> *To each other linked are,*
> *That thou canst not stir a flower*
> *Without troubling of a star.*

Our own contact with the angels can come more readily when we desire to work with them in the service of humanity, and when we feel a deep interconnectedness with all life. But our service, our thoughts for the world, need also to be positive and full of hope—and, as we saw in the last chapter, grounded in peaceful equanimity of being. If we were simply swayed by our emotions then we might be unwise or inappropriate in our giving. Ideally, we would have the kind of poise and awareness of the divine plan which allows us joyfully to serve the true need—the soul need—which the angels serve. The angels themselves bring a feeling of lightness of heart and true joy. They live totally in the awareness of the divine plan. They see the good developing within all life and nothing being outside of this.

* *The mantram 'Aum mani padme hum' which White Eagle has given us, which is learned at a certain stage in meditation classes, is attributed to Avalokitesvara. (Using a mantram in meditation is best done under direction.) The motto of the Lodge from its earliest days has been 'I serve', and people are invited from the first to join with the angels in the service of sending out the light. This is described later in this book in the section on White Eagle's healing prayer.*

Knowing this plan so intimately must mean that they live in divine joy—the true bliss which comes with such deep knowledge of how things truly are. We too can regain that sense of joy within ourselves, through developing our own trust in God's plan for our lives, and it will bring us closer to the angels.

This degree of trust is an essential element in our service, for without it, it is much harder to serve unemotionally. When difficult things happen, we all tend to be caught up in our own emotional responses. The flow of unconditional love to the situation is then inhibited, simply because we feel so sad, or so despairing for others. That is not to say that our feelings cannot be used, because paradoxically an emotional response can also be the trigger for our compassion. It can bring a desire to serve others and to help alleviate suffering through working with the angels to bring healing and peace. But if we also believe in the rightness of the plan, then we develop the kind of equanimity and surety which knows no limitations to that healing. We know that the angels, God's messengers, will bring good out of seeming chaos, light out of the darkness, and that knowing brings great power for good.

The following personal story, from my husband Jeremy Hayward, may make this understanding clearer for us. He is writing about an experience he had on holiday in Dorset one January:

'We were walking one of the hills that rises up behind the low sandstone cliffs by the sea. It is a popular place, with quite a large National Trust car park on the top. But on that January day, with occasional weak sunshine blotted out by misty clouds blowing in off the sea, there were very few of us on the hilltop—and indeed it didn't seem a specially inviting place to be, either.

'We dropped down off the top through the fields to the cliff edge, and because there was no way down to the shore, we decided to follow the edge and then make our way back up a farther spur of the hill. As we climbed we looked down into the valley folds where we had been. The wind was blowing in our faces and off the sea. I was so aware of the scents in the wind; the sharp freshness and purity of the air coming straight in off the sea. There was also the smell of damp earth and vegetation. (I couldn't help catching, too, the whiff of some fairly raunchy manure being spread by a tractor in the fields below.) I found myself thinking how in Native American days—when there was less intellectual development, but surely far more ability to receive and feel through the senses—such a wind would have been full of messages and stories, telling the perceiver much about the country around. Surely also, in this refinement of the senses, he or she would be able to feel keenly the subtler life behind the physical, just as I could more dimly feel something pure, even holy, in the tangy wind coming off the sea.

'I think it was because of this daydream that I was suddenly aware that I was touching a life behind the physical scene—which I was already drinking in with renewed delight. I knew I was touching, feeling, the life of the hill; but this life was also a consciousness and I was—as it were—just touching the hem of its garment. If this sounds dramatic, it wasn't really; but I was aware, almost underneath my thoughts, of this fount of light and joy which I can only call the angel of the hill. To a degree I could tell myself that the very folds and undulations of the hill were the body of this consciousness, but of course it was not really corporeal at all, and the consciousness felt at one, too, with the sharp air and the clouds. But the contact brought a great feeling of upliftment; it was even a contact with something majestic, and I felt that it reconnected me, in a humbling way, with my own heart. And still looking out on the landscape for those few moments, the constructions of human beings—the roads, the car park and huts half a mile away on the ridge, the new bypass I knew lay out of sight just inland—all felt beside the point, unimportant accretions on what was really there.

'Another thing I knew, again quite subtly and undramatically, was

that the consciousness which was the angel of the hill was totally
indifferent to whether it was, in human terms, a "nice day". Or rather,
I could say, it took equal delight either in fair weather or when, as
now, misty clouds and a faint cold drizzle were closing in from the
sea; it was equally fed by both. This moment of sharing in a life
beyond my own was a great gift, unexpected and not deliberately
sought. I have tried to describe the contact in mental terms, but what
it left me with was a deep feeling of wellbeing and healing. As we
walked slowly back across the top to the car, I found my heart felt
touched by every fold in the hills.

'Looking back on that walk in January, two things stand out for
me. The first is how much for the rest of the day every contour of
the land seemed to hold meaning. In an unsentimental way I felt I
had been told how precious the earth and its landscape is. The second thing is the deep impression left with me of how the angel truly
seemed to feel equal joy in all the different weathers surrounding the
hill, so differently from our ordinary human habits.

'It has made me think how much we can, perhaps unconsciously,
cling to things turning out for us in a certain way. This can be at all
levels. Our society places great stress, in perhaps a rather superficial
way, on freedom of choice. Of course it is a wonderful thing, but
when our choosing is done just from the outer self we can come to
feel that our happiness is dependent on certain material things being
in our lives, and this can then be a cause of pain. Surely this is what
some eastern teaching about "non-attachment" means: not that we
should not be able to enjoy fully every aspect of life on the physical
plane, but that if we believe we can only be happy if particular desires are met, then sometimes experiences come along which simply
remove our hands from holding, and teach us that the source of
happiness lies somewhere deeper. The same thing can be true at an
emotional level. We may believe that only if our children are doing
well at school, and we have a good job, and our partner is being

unstintingly sympathetic to us and agreeing with our way of seeing things, and so on, can we be really happy.

'And I think we can cling at a spiritual level too. We can so much wish for everything to be outwardly perfect that if negative, angry or unruly emotions should come in, we feel threatened—and then they actually loom far larger than they warrant. The lesson I felt the moment of communion with the angel of the hill brought to me was the reverse of all this; it was a glimpse of a deep equanimity.

'It was as if the angel lived forever in the realization, "*Whatever* happens—all is well now". Aware, for a moment, with the angel, I felt that nothing in life needed to be resisted. Even in pain or suffering, one's heart, if not one's mind, could know: "All is well now". Even in looking on apparently distressing incidents in the world, one could give greater love, greater healing, by starting deep from the stillness of the same understanding, "All is well—all is part of a great process of unfoldment to the light". White Eagle says: "Bear always in mind, in your ardour to do work for the upliftment of humanity, that love is your implement. This means that you must be at peace; you must be content to see error, even suffering, with a calm mind. For love will teach you that behind this outer manifestation of chaotic humanity there is the light, which is the love and wisdom of God, your Father–Mother".'

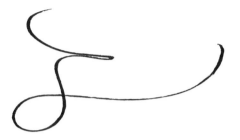

4. The Power of the Holy Breath

One of the ways in which we can calm our nervous system, and gain the kind of poise of being which White Eagle describes, is through conscious God-breathing. At the same time, this practice of consciously breathing in light and breathing forth love, is, as you will read from White Eagle, a beautiful way of serving.

God-breathing enables us both to strengthen and sensitize the etheric connection so as to feel the presence of the angels in the ether. It also strengthens the nervous system so that it may respond with compassion in the most balanced of ways. White Eagle has given us a great deal of instruction about how to do this.

If you could only realize fully the meaning of 'Breathe on me, breath of God....' Breathe *in* me breath of God. Every person, every moment of their lives is breathing in God's life, without which they could not continue to live in a physical body; for it is not only air that you are breathing into your lungs, you are absorbing all the goodness and beauty and harmony which is in God's life. We wonder how many on earth realize its power, which is that of life, of wisdom and of love. You breathe in the white light, and in the white light are all the colours made perfect in one....

Notice the power there is in this breathing-in of life. You breathe in—you say, automatically: do so now with thankfulness and peace, for then you breathe in the love of God, which is the life of the universe. You live and have your being in this universal life.

He adds, in a passage familiar to readers of PRAYER IN THE NEW AGE:

We often speak to you of 'breathing in the holy breath'. What is the holy breath? It is harmony. When you try to breathe in the breath of God you are breathing in harmony, healing; for the way you perform this simple act can affect your whole life—your spiritual unfoldment and your physical, mental and spiritual health. At this moment, relax your mind and body, and breathe deeply, quietly and slowly. As you breathe in, try to imagine that you are breathing in light and life; that you are not only inhaling air, you are filling every particle of your being with God's breath. As you do this you will naturally be freed from the problems that constrict you, because your whole mind will be on God. You will also find relief from the bondage of cares and limitations if you will practise this deep 'God-breathing'; it will bring you a sense of peace, poise and control.

As you breathe, slowly, rhythmically, calmly, at the same time forgetting the earth, raise your thoughts, your aspiration to the world above, the world of spirit. Breathe in the fragrance of the rose. Breathe in the light of God. Breathe out the love of God. Be still and know God. Peace ... peace ... be still.

Because the conscious breath is the link between the etheric and the physical body, and because it affects all the subtle bodies, it brings peace and balance to the nervous system. Using the conscious breath allows you to be attuned to the inner worlds in a more harmonious way. Indeed, you are drawing closer into contact with the angels. White Eagle (in SUN-MEN OF THE AMERICAS) has this to say about the way of life of the Native Americans as he knew it: 'They were taught … how in the act of breathing in the fresh air they could also establish contact with the angels of light.' And he relates the sense of smell to the element earth, and says that when this sense is developed more fully, the finer essences of life within the earth can be detected:

> You can, if you will, smell the fragrance, the life, the very essence of the earth; and you can penetrate even beyond this to absorb or inhale the essence of the cosmic body. Do you see what this means? Through your physical sense of smell, you may penetrate into the life of God.
>
> This rhythmic breathing does something more than affect your body. Seen clairvoyantly, the person who in full consciousness breathes in the divine life is radiating a great light. He or she is strengthening the soul and causing it to expand and send out feelers of light, shafts of light. You breathe in and absorb this stream of life and light from the Father– Mother God, and then you let it fall from you in blessing upon others. So you absorb God's life, and you bless all life. You receive and you give; and so you come into harmony with the rhythmic lifestream. It will feed your nerves, and give you a sense of peace and control.
>
> Conscious breathing in this way has the effect of harmonizing the channel to the divine, to God, to the innermost, the centre within. By your slowing down the breathing, and breathing the God-life, the whole being is harmonized and the divine energy is brought forth. Breathing can link up the three centres, the heart, the throat and the head. When the

three centres are brought into complete at-one-ment, perfect harmony exists and then the projection goes forth with great power. And as the projection goes forth, let it do so on a breath of God. You breathe in divine energy, you breathe out, or project, the breath of God—the divine breath to bless and to heal.

If you follow our exercises you will find wellbeing will result, and no harm, but only good. As you breathe rhythmically and deeply you are affecting the mental and astral bodies, and all the higher bodies are affected thereby. It must be the breath of the divine life which you are breathing. You must keep your spine straight, because the forces travel up the centre of the body. It is not good to try, in the early stages, to breathe too deeply, or to hold the breath, causing the heart to palpitate and the head to go light. It is not good to breathe in a strained way. All breathing should be harmonious and give you no discomfort. You must breathe slowly, quietly, harmoniously; gradually getting the breath deeper until you are filling and emptying the lower part of the lungs and expanding the ribs as you breathe. It must come gradually.

Stand, if possible (or sit or lie) before an open window, or go into the open air. As you inhale each breath, aspire to God—feel that God is entering into you; as you exhale bless all life. This inbreathing will cause spiritual light, light from the spiritual Sun behind the physical sun, to enter into you and register on the membranes at the head centre, on the brow. From that centre you can mentally direct the light to the heart centre. In this way you can bring spiritual water and sunlight to the seed atom which rests in the human heart. If you feel this divine fire in your heart it will come as strength. It will be to you like a rod of light (the straight spine). If when weary and tired physically you practise your yogic breathing you will find yourself charged with vitality and will not know weariness.

White Eagle often helps us to use this God-breathing as a means of making a meditative contact of the deepest kind. He says,

We ask you to practise the holy breathing, the slow, rhythmic, calm, relaxed breathing; and, at the same time, forgetting the earth, to rise in aspiration to the world above, the world of spirit life, which is a world of light where all souls live in the full consciousness of the true life, the God-life. For there the people walk and talk with angels. We want you to aspire: to look up into the mountain heights. We want you to visualize an immense mountain peak which reaches upward almost beyond your vision. The peak of the mountain we want you to visualize as the throne of the king of kings, of the Lord Christ, and we want you to see him enthroned in a great circle of light. In that circle of light are countless angelic forms, and from that great Star circle there is a radiation extending for an immense distance.

Perhaps, if we follow what White Eagle says, we do not so much breathe as let the breath breathe us. When we let the spirit breathe within us and around us we are part of the great ocean of God's life, and as White Eagle says elsewhere we do not hold the world up; rather, God holds the world up. We do not breathe alone, isolated in our body of flesh; we breathe with all life, with the whole earth and cosmos, and we are aware that God breathes in us and with us.

5. Time for Stillness and Silence

White Eagle says:

The first step towards becoming aware is to gain a condition of stillness, of peace, of tranquillity. Unless you can enter into this silent chamber, you cannot approach the gateway which lies concealed within, and which opens upon the great garden of life, unlimited and eternal.

In the process of your development you discard the veils which shield you from this vast array of spiritual power. Eye hath not seen, ear hath not heard, the glories that are prepared for the person who reaches heaven. This is your future and this is worth striving for. When you are distracted by material things keep very calm, keep very still. Remember the brethren of the silence, whose very power of achievement lies in silence. Touch the silence, and the power of the spirit will flow into you and disperse all your fears. Nothing is so important as God, and until you have developed the required spiritual qualities, and touch this profound spiritual silence, you will find it hard to penetrate the finer ethers.

The approach towards this profound silence is not merely a matter of being quiet, or being in a quiet place, though this obviously does help. But it is the condition of stillness and silence one creates within oneself which unlocks the door to that 'unlimited and eternal' garden where the angels dwell. The inner stillness one seeks to create is one of receptivity. It is one of laying aside the opinions, problems, habits of thought and emotions of the earth. More than this, it is one of emptying the mind of self, much as one would pour out the old contents of a cup, and leave it clear for the spirit to flow in and fill it.

Inner stillness can be developed within ourselves throughout daily life, as well as in times of meditation, through a degree of watchfulness. Besides mentioning the brethren of the silence, White Eagle refers to the great angels at the head of the seven rays—the Elohim— as the silent watchers.* Watchfulness, in this context, means a patient, waiting regard towards life. Too often we can tend to rush forward with actions or words, or critical thoughts, when later and with time we can see a wider picture which changes our perception of things. Too often, in meditation, we become impatient because we cannot 'see', or don't appear to 'get anything'. Instead, an attitude of patient, open waiting and watching within eventually produces such a feeling of desireless peace and stillness that we automatically and without striving 'discard the veils which shield us'. It is a process which will happen naturally if we create the right conditions.

Part of this watchfulness in daily life lies in respecting the need for silence and stillness, so that we live our lives with energy and enthusiasm balanced by stillness and quiet. Such times of silence are important, and for some people vital. No matter the constraints of our home circumstances, it is possible to take ourselves away for a few minutes of quiet. This may not even be in meditation, but simply walking in the garden or the park, sitting in a quiet room in the house, the local library or church. It may simply lie in asking kindly for some peace.

*There is more about the silent watchers on p. 93 of this book.

In the following passages White Eagle describes the kind of contact with the spirit which was made by the Native Americans long ago. We may not be able to take ourselves off to the mountaintops, but the picture does convey how particular times of day and phases of the moon can be more auspicious.

We lay special emphasis on the time when you are all most close to that life behind the veil, which is just before sleep at night or at any time when you quieten all outer noise and mental activity—when you become subdued. You can do this by centring your heart upon the gentle spirit of Christ and God the Mother–Father. Great activity and development can take place for you during the sleeping of the physical body; the ancients well knew the activity which took place at the time of the setting sun and all through those quiet hours until the rising sun.

So also at the time of the full moon, the silver moon which the ancients regarded as the symbol of the higher mind or the intellect, there came a hush of quiet waiting. In the long ago we perambulated the great mountain places in prayer and silence, except for the rhythmic tread of human feet. Under the silver moon we waited expectantly, until there came the breaking of the golden dawn. Then the golden rays impregnated the silver.

This is a great mystical truth concerned with development in your being. It is something for which everyone must work in themselves. The intellect has to become stilled and ready to assimilate truth—has to rise to a certain level of understanding. At that level it is ready to receive the impregnation of the golden rays of the Sun or of the spirit, so the soul and the spirit meet.

This ancient rite or ritual has come down right through

the ages from a distant past and is still held, at the inner level, in Britain, at that holy place called Stonehenge.* Once you have reached a certain stage of development the curtain of the mists will be swept aside. Then will you see the glory of that rising Sun and the company of the great beings, the angels—of ageless beings waiting to welcome you into this newborn spiritual day. Do not think that you are far removed from such a grand spiritual experience, such ecstasy of being. You are not. Day by day you are approaching this illumination, for which you must prepare in mind and in heart.

Understand this, that before you rest each night you should prepare yourselves to go forth from your body into that higher ether. There you will undergo spiritual experiences which will so impress the mind that you will waken in the morning with a gentle memory of something wonderful having happened. In this preparation for sleep and the way you sleep, you are training yourselves to receive divine illumination and freedom from the chains and bondage of earthly life.

When you fall asleep let your mind be calm and still. Think of the hush over the earth. All nature sleeps. Put yourself into rhythm with nature. In like manner all nature awaits the coming, the baptism of the sun. Then will you be released harmoniously and your guardian angel at your side will take your hand and lead you forth to one of the many temples that exist on the etheric plane; and there you will receive instruction, and your soul will be impressed so vividly that some of the experiences will remain in your waking moments.

---

* *There is more about Stonehenge and the ceremonies enacted there in chapter 21, which is on ritual, ceremonial and sacred places. See also Grace and Ivan Cooke, THE LIGHT IN BRITAIN (White Eagle Publishing Trust, 1971).*

Picture the angelic beings singing and praising God for the glory of the fuller life, the beauty of the worlds invisible. Through stillness and quietness surrender yourselves. Relax in sleep and you, your true self, will go forth free to take your place in the world of light. There you may learn, and reach and instruct those people on the earth to whom you are attached, and who need the help which you can give.

The following are more of White Eagle's words, and form a meditation on silence.

In the beginning was the Word, and the Word came from the heart of silence, from the stillness of life. Silence is power. Life becomes active in the silence when the word of God goes forth.

Noise, discord, is disruptive, disintegrating. And remember, the mind can make as much noise as the mouth.

Meditate on the stillness of God....

Thus the light radiates from you, and thus you carry the rays of healing and peace.

6. The Chakras: Bridge to the Etheric World

When White Eagle describes the chakra system he chooses not to go into great occult detail, but on one occasion he gave an outline that I find particularly helpful and inspiring.

He described the angelic presences who gather in the silence of a sanctuary. Besides giving a most beautiful account of the angels themselves, his teaching on that occasion also covered the development of the chakras. These are vortices of power within the etheric body, connected to the main ganglions of nerves in the physical body. Through the chakras the soul qualities manifest. White Eagle shows us that it is through the opening and development of the chakras in meditation, as well as through loving service in daily life, that the ability to experience the angelic presence comes about.

> We speak of the angels and devas: this little sanctuary is charged, particularly tonight, with the pure white light. Had you eyes to see, you would see. In front of the pituitary gland is the 'eye'* which registers the vibrations of the next step, of the etheric plane. The physical eye is aware only of the vibrations of physical light, but the brow chakra with the

* *White Eagle is referring to the chakra situated between the eyebrows.*

pituitary gland reflects the etheric light; and you should, when you focus your attention there, become aware of light, and then of colour. All the most delicate colours of the rainbow are here. Having been trained, each one of you can, by closing your eyes and letting the outer senses fall into abeyance, reflect the vibrations of colour on the etheric plane. You will see the most delicate colours of the rainbow, moving, vibrating, in beautifully soft, billow-like clouds; and see beings standing with folded wings all around this sanctuary. They are still and they are directing rays of light, which go forth from their auras.

We would draw your attention to the seven planes of life, or degrees of vibration. These are linked to the present being of a person in the physical body through the chakras; centres of power which are attached to the lower etheric body and also to the spinal column, and are the receiving stations for the vital force. Only through these centres and the etheric body to which they are connected does the body maintain its life-force. Also, this etheric body is a bridge—it is that part of a person which enables contact to be made with higher worlds—between the physical and the spirit.

Connecting again with the dense etheric body is the finer etheric body, a body of light. This is the soul body, which has its own quality of consciousness, and is a creation not of physical birth, but of long ages past. In this soul body we find woven the experiences of the past, the higher worlds, the higher planes of being.

You have learnt of the pituitary gland, situated behind and between the two eyes; this is linked with the pineal gland near the cerebellum, and it is through these two centres that the soul consciousness is maintained. These two glands are attached to the psychic centres (chakras) in the head, and in the course of development they will meet. Then the crown centre will be fully opened and there will be complete soul consciousness. Pictures of the Lord Buddha showing development at the crown of the head suggest that here was the awakening of that all-important head centre.

The soul consciousness manifests through the head chakras. Yet the divine spirit dwells in the heart. The heart chakra is the central power station, so that when the spiritual force, or love, is flowing into the heart centre, that force flows on into the other chakras and they light up.

In the White Eagle Lodge we work on one specific ray to help each other to rise above the limitations of the earth. Step by step this is taking place, but so imperceptibly in us all that it is not apparent, except perhaps in the atmosphere (which may be felt as a loving atmosphere), because the one foundation on which the God-powers can be built is that of devotion, of love. Through these the heart chakra opens and the light streams forth from the heart.... The light from the heart stimulates the serpent power [the creative power at the base of the spine], and as this power rises it stimulates [that is, illumines] all the other centres of the body.

The safe and correct way for spiritual unfoldment is to work from the heart of love. In your meditation you are being taught how to bring these higher chakras to life, how to open your consciousness to the pure, the spiritual level of life. The right way to unfold the inner faculties is through developing the sixth sense, or intuition, which functions from the heart centre. In true meditation, in true contemplation of God and all that is holy, you are opening the heart centre. In meditation you become very conscious at all times of divine will to control the emotions and direct them wisely— not to repress them but to raise them onto a higher plane of love and service and kindness. This daily meditation is the true path of the spiritual unfoldment of the powers of clear vision and clear hearing. The power is then controlled in the solar plexus; it is stimulated in the heart, the throat and the head; it is directed at all times by the divine will in the heart.

The unfoldment of the chakras can be quickened by love, but the development of love without knowledge is not enough. It is necessary to develop the wisdom aspect, and to strive for full consciousness of what you are doing on these higher planes. We know that all things can be done with love, but if you do not get knowledge love can be compared to the flower which has not opened. Love is also wisdom, and to love you must be wise because you can give the greatest amount of help to others by wisdom as well as by love. As an illustration take a mother's love for her child, which will be apparently unselfish. The mother can give and give and give of her love until the child is utterly ruined. Is that love unselfish, or is it only self-indulgence? To love truly you will put the good of others first—the true good, the real spiritual advantage. You are giving that which will help other souls to develop their love and their Godlike qualities too.

It is interesting that at the end of this passage White Eagle brings us back to the selfless, dispassionate love—the pure love, as he calls it—of the angels. It is clear that he does not advocate the direct stimulation and development of the chakras. Rather, he gives us the picture of how through our personal self-discipline, and concentration on the love and wisdom of the heart, all the other chakras will be balanced and developed in the most natural and harmonious way.

His description of the degree of spiritual awareness and vision which are reached as the chakras naturally and gently open—through meditation and through wise love expressed in our daily lives—is also beautiful. As always White Eagle emphasizes that all spiritual unfoldment begins with 'scrubbing the floor of our own lodge' (one of his best-known phrases). It is in working at the challenges of our human life that we find attunement to the inner worlds.

It is your reactions to daily events and to the conditions of life that really bring about attunement, achievement. It is no good listening to White Eagle or to any other teacher unless you yourself work for self-mastery. The beginning of this work is your awareness of the 'still small voice' within, of that gradually increasing light in you which causes you to react as a gentle brother to all the conditions and all the circumstances of life.

Thus your eyes can be opened, for example, to the seething millions of etheric forms which exist in the ethers interpenetrating the earth, and the way to open the vision and awaken the consciousness is through quiet meditation. By meditation we mean a going *beneath* all thought to the level of spiritual life, and becoming aware of the light and the power which is, in a very fine degree at first, like an electric current in you.

This is the light of the spirit, the power which slowly and gradually becomes aroused in your physical body and moves right up into your head. It is what the ancient sages called the solar force. This solar force must never be stimulated until the individual is earnestly seeking the truth and the life of Christ, and not for selfish motives, or to satisfy curiosity. The beginning of this stimulation lies in prayer and meditation.

When you have, in this way, developed a degree of sensitivity through the development of the light within, you react in greater degree to the influence of the spiritual Sun.

Through the sensitive nervous system the consciousness of the brain is opened—the eyes of the spiritual body are opened. When you have really gained mastery over the physical body, the nervous system and the thinking—so that in all ways you can create the condition that the divine will within you wishes to create—then you are able, when you sit in meditation, to build round you 'the temple of the golden flower', exquisitely formed of spiritual or celestial substance. In meditation you are fully open like a beautiful flower: like the thousand-petalled lotus of the head chakra, or the many-petalled lotus of the heart chakra. You as a spirit are actually in that flower, and that flower builds up all around you in the form of a most beautiful temple, a spiritual temple. You are then in the temple of your own soul and spiritual world.

7. In Touch with Nature

The angels keep their ancient places;—
Turn but a stone and start a wing!
'Tis ye, 'tis your estrangèd faces,
That miss the many-splendoured thing.

FRANCIS THOMPSON

It is not by chance that we find White Eagle referring again and again to the natural world. He has provided us with many descriptions of the intimate relationship that the Native American, for example, had and still has with mother earth and her creatures, and how that contact was the basis of the 'red man's' spiritual growth and power. Furthermore White Eagle has shown us how a deeper contact with the etheric world is brought about through putting ourselves *en rapport* with the rhythms of nature.

White Eagle says that the angels are intimately connected to the world of nature and the animal kingdom under the direction of divine Mother, in ways which we cannot conceive with the limited earthly mind. He has taught us more and more to develop this contact with nature if we wish to work with the angelic beings, as did the ancient peoples, to bring healing to the earth, and to further the manifestation of the light within the earth. In the following passages

(one of them previously printed in the book SPIRITUAL UNFOLDMENT
II) he gives us very lovely descriptions of this intimate relationship
between nature and the angels, which show how important it is for
us to feel our oneness with the natural world and the etheric life
within it.

The materialist has his or her place in the grand scheme of
evolution. Such people bring to humanity a power, a driving force, which eventually causes the opening of the higher
mind. For out of that compelling hunger is born another
urge, the urge of love: the urge to make contact with something not previously understood, but which a person feels,
through a slowly awakening intuition, that he or she needs.

People as a whole do not always desire to love, to give
love, but they do desire to *be* loved. From this suppressed
flame within all is born a desire to understand that which is
invisible, but can yet be sensed and felt. For the mind tells
them, when they look forth upon an awakening spring, when
they listen to gentle and grand music, when they wonder at
a sunset or the brilliance of a starlit night, that behind these
manifestations of beauty there must be a power: perhaps a
mind, an intellect which has caused all, the power of which
strikes an harmonious note within the breast. For not only
the beauty of colour and form, the majesty of nature, but
some vibration invisible and behind the physical manifestation, brings harmony to the soul.

It is through Christ in you that you are able to recognize
the beautiful nature spirits behind all physical forms, all sen-
tient life. To this grand brotherhood of nature we would
open your eyes, for you must in due course learn to call
upon the service of the brotherhood of the angelic kingdom. This present age of Aquarius will bring the angelic

and the nature kingdom closer to the human.

The master who directs and guides the work of the White Eagle Lodge was most enlightened and trained in the work of making contact with the elementals, the nature spirits, the angels. You are all evolving towards this and you can help yourselves and all beings, the animals, flowers and all nature, by becoming simple as children. Do not think we decry the development of the intellect, because through the intellect humanity will be able to comprehend more fully these wonderful forms of life and states of life. But the way you can help yourselves and the whole world to evolve towards that state of brotherhood between human kind and the angels is by endeavouring, as you look on any physical form, to look *into* that form and see the spirit working.

Try to look through outer form to see the spirit form within or behind the physical. For instance, when you are meditating, you may see stones or rocks. Try to penetrate these rocks with your inner vision. Then you will find yourself in a fairy world, in an Aladdin's cave, and you will see the stones shine like jewels, rare and beautiful in colour and texture. As the aspirant advances she or he learns that the mineral kingdom is far from inanimate: it is pulsating with life, and even, to a certain degree, with intelligence—something which is perhaps not comprehensible to the human mind. You do not yet realize what a world of beauty lies hidden within the world of physical matter! The true clairvoyant has the joy of seeing this beauty revealed.

See it in the very roots of the trees, in the trunk, branches and the leaves. See the white light rising as the sap rises. See this phenomenon taking place in the flowers and bushes and trees and all nature. Look always for the spirit behind or within all form. Become *en rapport* with this spiritual God-life in everything you see. Realize it in the air you breathe, in the water you drink and bathe in. See it in the sky, in the winds, in the air; see it in the fire. Cultivate this inner gift; call it, if you like, imagination, but remember that imagination is the bridge which will take you across physical matter into the etheric and indeed into the celestial world. By using this gift you can help yourselves and all humanity. It will create harmony in yourselves and beauty in your lives, for you will have realms revealed to you that you do not know exist at the present time....

The earth is not dark as is usually supposed, but is full of fire and light.

The Beauty and Sacredness of Trees

In the following passages White Eagle puts into words the delight which is to be found in the majesty and beauty of nature. He demonstrates where the joy we feel comes from: he says that in our delight we are responding, albeit often unconsciously, to the presence of the angels.

You may not have realized before what an important place the nature world holds in the grand scheme of life. We are conscious of the beauty of trees, and many love to be alone and walk under the trees, or sit beneath, and contemplate the sunlight and dream of life made radiant and beautiful. Even then you may not become fully aware of the pulsating life behind, beneath and above those trees. A tree may mean no more to you than a tree. But through aspiration and attunement you can be released from bondage, and see with the eye of truth and illumination the interblending of all life, the companies of angels, of nature spirits and of devas, and thus become yourself recreated and rejuvenated. In this new world you are conscious of a light which surrounds and permeates all those living, moving atoms of life.

The trees enfold humanity as a mother; the trees are symbolic of the great Mother. Realizing this, we can walk in the groves, sit beneath the great oaks, or an ancient banyan, or the majesty of the cedar, and become conscious of this divine mother-love enfolding us.

The sages of old chose the trees as their cathedrals. Can you not recognize in the pillar and arch and groyne of the cathedral or palace, a symbol or a replica of the fundamental principles of the structure of a tree? In some quiet woodland—veritably a natural cathedral—have you not felt the sense of love and peace, and registered the blessing of those natural sanctuaries? There are many such cathedrals built by the tree spirits on the astral plane of life, where many weary souls coming from the earth can find refreshment and worship, not by word, but through the adoration and thankfulness of their hearts.

In ancient days before there were stone temples, the simple brethren congregated on a high plain or hilltop, and although trees are not frequently found at such a height, in spirit we can take you to such a temple of trees. There you will see these immense trees like pillars of verdant green. You will see the tall aisle or nave, which is built from the sweeping, graceful branches of the trees, and the light of the spiritual Sun shining onto the leaves which move gently in the breeze. In that sunlight, if you look very closely with your heart as well as your higher mind, you will see the countless forms of the sun spirits and the little sylphs in the gentle breeze. You will also notice that the trees form a natural temple—a natural, graceful structure, filled with the myriad spirits of the sun and the air and the earth—the spirits of the earth rising from the earth and becoming active on the green carpet which covers the arena. Here, in your meditations, you will get the feeling of the brotherhood of life, hear the song of the birds, smell the sweetness of all nature— here in this temple at the heart of heaven.

The sacred rites the ancients performed show forth the knowledge and wisdom handed down from the God-people and the angel visitants from other planetary spheres. We ourselves are conscious of having once participated in some of these grand and ancient rites in a pine-clad district of our land. In company with our brethren, we have remained many days and nights watching the sun reborn behind the pine trees it then irradiates. We have seen it rise into the heavens, and in silence and prayer and contemplation, seen it disappear as a ball of gold behind the pines. We have been taught that those same pines were symbolical of the birth of the Sun—not only the sun terrestrial, but the celestial Son, even Christ.

On another occasion, White Eagle gave a description of his times of rest in the spirit world, demonstrating how important the contact with nature, and in this case, the trees, can be—even when one has passed into the world of light:

Just as you put your body to rest on a couch at night, so we too pass into the halls of slumber. On one occasion we withdrew from the sheath we continually use to contact the earth and laid it down on a mossy bank amid pine trees—for pine trees have for us a particular significance; they are part of this very sheath we use. The very vehicle we use is harmonized with nature, with the pine trees, with the canopy of heaven and the stars. And the world became dim to us, and the sheath which we used slept under the pines.

Just as your physical body can rest, and while in that resting state absorb light and strength from the surroundings, so our vehicle, which is adapted to the work on the physical plane, sometimes needs rest and restoration. But that vehicle is not ourselves. We are separate from that body, we are free.

And so in this condition it rested, absorbing the beauty of the life-force of those pine trees in the spirit world.

Perhaps in this description of White Eagle's relationship with the pine trees, a glimpse is given of what it can mean to feel 'at one' with the natural world in a very deep sense; a oneness of being where the limitations of physical life are dissolved, and the soul is free to absorb and be absorbed in all creation. People have reported experiencing this state of consciousness whilst in nature, perhaps somewhere not often frequented by others. It is also an experience we can have in meditation, a state in which it is possible to be aware of the body, and at the same time aware of our intimate connection with life.

Contemplating the Sea

When talking about the special quality of divine Mother which walking amongst the trees can bring, White Eagle contrasted this with the sense of power which comes from observing the sea.

Contemplating the sea will reveal to your soul a new meaning. The sea may lie still and quiet while, standing alone in some quiet place, your soul can reach out and become conscious of the vastness, the depth and the profundity of life. Your frail earthly comprehension reels with the magnificence of the stillness and power of the sea.

Let us visualize these oceans: let us feel the motion, the life of the sea … joy abounding; see the clearness of the water and the sunlight upon it. Identify yourselves with brother sea and brother air and brother sun.… May the ocean speak to you of the eternal powers which lie within the creation of the universe; the waters enfold humanity in an enveloping, yet impersonal peace.… They hold you all in an immense power.

Birds and Angels

White Eagle has said that the angels are particularly connected with the air element. Of all the animal kingdom, it is the birds who are therefore closest to the angels, since they are masters of the air, and free in this element. For example, there are many remarkable stories of the distances birds can fly—like the young swift which, we are told, will not touch the ground for three years after it is born! There are other links between the angels and the birds, too. White Eagle says:

In ancient mythology a bird conveyed the idea of an angelic messenger, and also symbolized a certain aspect in the soul. Thus birds played a great part in teaching people of these heavenly qualities. Many an aspirant to spiritual wisdom would spend long hours listening to the song of birds, studying their habits and learning to interpret their language.

The song of the birds touches hidden vibrations within you which can respond to heavenly influences. These can be played upon by the heavenly forces, and the song can help to strengthen and bring into human consciousness that aspect of the heavenly life with which it is in harmony.

The birds bring happiness, they release your soul into spiritual realms. You cannot help being happy when you hear the song of birds. Listening to birdsong a chord awakens in you which carries you into the spiritual worlds. Do not listen with the mind alone, but the chords of the heart should be struck by the sound—and then you are released. You fly; you overcome earthiness like birds. Even in the spirit world, when the soul first comes over, it finds itself in very lovely natural surroundings, sometimes in a beautiful sunlit garden, among birds of beautiful plumage and colouring. Or the soul will find a lovely sunlit wood, and spend long periods communing with the birds, and the spirit birds will sit upon the person's shoulders.

The songs of the birds are also the vibrations which assist the nature spirits to bring forth the fruits of the earth. Train yourself, when you are in the woodland, to shut out all earthly sounds, and enter into the innermost in yourself: you will then hear sounds, harmonies—not only the deep musical harmony of nature, but nature *within* nature. In that music, nature spirits have being; these sounds quicken their life-force, and enable them to receive instruction from the one at the head of the ray upon which they live.

Birds, then, are symbolical of soul qualities: streams of life-force from the Godhead, and therefore they form a link between humanity and God. When birds die they are reborn into etheric bodies in the nature kingdom. They are reborn (without our being too definite) as the little people who populate the etheric worlds, whose work behind the veil of matter is to assist in the growth of flowers and bushes and trees. The birds share in this nature kingdom, and, as they evolve—it takes a long time—they become spirits of the air, or spirits of the fire, or spirits of the great seas. Eventually they become what are called angels or devas, and continue to evolve until they pass through solar initiation and become planetary beings.

Thus you will see that some angels, according to the lifestream* upon which they have been sent forth from the heart of God, evolve through bird life, through the nature kingdom, before they take their place in the great heavenly hosts who watch over humanity.

Reading these words of White Eagle helped me realize why birdsong is so evocative and joyous for many people. I recalled how at the beginning of the age of Aquarius (an air sign) there seems everywhere to be a growing awareness of the importance of the angelic life and of the need to conserve our natural world. This awareness of spiritual science, I think, is just as important a part of the true 'Aquarian' as empirical science and mental development. Indeed it will be the growing understanding and inner knowledge of our true relationship with nature and the angels which will bring the greatest scientific discoveries and inventions as the age advances. My feeling was that unless it goes to this level of awareness, science would stagnate; that this is the next step.

As I write I am particularly aware of the work done at the White Eagle Centre for the Americas in Texas. The centre is well known in the local community not only for its spiritual work but for the rescue and rehabilitation work done there with injured birds (particularly raptors). I am sure that the helpers there would say that

* *The theme of the different lifestreams is continued in chapter 14.*

the birds bring a great deal to the centre too, both emotionally and
spiritually.

Putting Oneself in Nature's Lifestream

White Eagle has told us that through our contact with nature we not
only learn to work with the angels, but also to balance and harmonize our physical bodies. He says that much of the disease, and certainly 'nerve strain' which we experience in our modern world is due
to our being 'shut away from this contact'. The Aquarian Age is the
age of the mind, and certainly the mental abilities and intelligence
of people is growing; but White Eagle would say that an overempha-
sis on the development of this air element means that we lose touch
with the healing, balancing powers of the other elements: earth, fire
and water. When it is out of balance the body becomes ill.

A friend of mine once had a very clear far memory of a life lived
as a Native American. He was aware of the strength and resilience
of his physical body then; the capacity he had for enduring pain
because every sense was open to the inner life of nature. He may
have been intellectually more simple, but his whole understanding
was deeper because the body was more open to the divine life and
vitality of the natural world. Through development of the physical
senses his etheric senses were tuned, and thus he contacted the spirit
within all life. In this way the lower chakras in the body, those more
concerned with water, fire and earth, were balanced with the higher
ones—with air and ether.*

In the following passage White Eagle continues to help us realize
the benefits of our contact with nature.

*This experience is certainly borne out when we read White Eagle's teaching on the Native
Americans in SUN-MEN OF THE AMERICAS.*

As you grow in awareness the flowers will speak to you. In every flower there is a vibration of God, and every flower has an affinity with some part of your organism. This the sages knew, and still know. Therefore they used flowers and herbs, as healing remedies; not only the material substance of the flower, but also its accompanying colour and planetary vibration. Each has its due effect upon some centre in the human organism. It is truly said that there is a herb for the cure of every disease. The little flower is the medium to receive its particular God-vibration; but a human being is the medium for the whole universe, and you contain within yourself *every* vibration in universal life.

During healing services in the Lodge, White Eagle has many times asked his healers to try and find time to be in natural surroundings, and to learn from the natural world, in order to allow the angels to work through them more readily when giving a healing treatment. White Eagle talks often about the Master Jesus, whom he calls the Great Healer, the being at the head of the healing ray. The following passage is taken from one of these talks.

Make no mistake: to become divine does not make you less human. Dear Jesus, we can assure you, was a most human and happy man, and a delightful companion. May we paint you a picture, which we should like you to carry forever in your memory?

A man who is full of the energy of life; a man who is untiring, who never wearies, who enjoys the companionship of his brethren, who enters into all the exercises and all the enjoyment of life: this, we assure you, is the nature of dear Jesus. He will plunge into the blue lake and swim effortlessly across and around and back and forth. He will enter the sphere of youth—with the young children—and will enjoy playing with them in their delightful garden of spring; playing with great balls, like your soap bubbles, so delicate and so airy and so full of colour and light. All manner of pursuits he will enter with all the God-zest in his soul. He will go amongst the young people and will enter into their interests, their exercises and their pursuits. Every aspect of life Jesus will love and will enjoy to the glory of his Creator.

We want you also to hold this zest for life, to enjoy life in all its forms and aspects. Learn to enter into the life of the animals, enjoying them and reading, from what you see with your spirit, their feelings. You know that animals have their own language, and it is up to the humans to try and learn it. The birds have their language and we in spirit have been initiated into this language. The etheric world, the nature kingdom, the salamanders, the sprites, the sylphs, all have their language and their music. And their language is understood by the soul who has so persevered along the God-path of life that she or he has become able quite clearly to understand the language of all forms of life. This may seem to you a very wide vista, but we speak thus to encourage you and to help you on your path.

8. A Brother Close to the Angels—Francis of Assisi

When I read White Eagle's teaching one of the things that most stands out is his emphasis on the interconnection of the natural world with the angelic stream of life. The plant and animal kingdoms are governed by the angels; and the link between the natural and the angelic is pure and simple, free from the interference, lack of understanding and wilfulness of humanity.

Besides the Master Jesus, whom White Eagle described so beautifully at the end of the last chapter, there have been other great souls who have allowed their bond with the natural world to flourish and deepen. Francis of Assisi has been one of the greatest examples to us of what such a contact can be like. Reading what White Eagle says about the connection between the birds and the angels gives us a picture of just how close to the angels Brother Francis was, and that the birds and other creatures responded to him because of this.

Some of you may recall a past incarnation when you dwelt with your brethren in a monastic life. We particularly wish to strike this note because we desire to draw to you the inspiration and the blessing of the gentle spirit of Francis of Assisi, a brother of an order closely linked to the heavenly and angelic life.

Different lifestreams manifest in different forms, but all fit into the grand pattern of evolution of physical life. It is not unusual for us to touch this angelic lifestream when we talk to you. We do this because at the present time it is what humanity needs—the vibration of the angelic life-forces—to restore humanity to its correct balance. The angels work unceasingly to uplift humanity, to prepare humanity for the coming of the Lord of this earth.

Francis of Assisi understood this grand brotherhood of life. Being raised above the human, he lived and expressed life on this angelic vibration. Because of this he attracted to himself the birds, which responded to his command; his spirit was speaking a bird language—akin, in lowly degree, to an angelic language.

Brother Francis was so attuned to the Great White Light that he could feel his brotherhood with all creatures and with all nature—with mother earth; sister water, brother air and brother sun. Francis had arrived at that full consciousness of brotherhood. Brother Francis and his helpers draw very close to stimulate compassion in people's hearts. Those who have eyes to see will see his radiant form with all the birds of the air around him. The white dove of peace flutters down from the great light above him, and these birds speak to you of love, of the Great White Spirit. We want you to remember this, and to do all you can to alleviate the suffering of animals on your earth plane. For we say most earnestly that until humanity refrains from cruelty to the brethren of the animal kingdom, and even to mother earth herself, as well as to the human kingdom, human beings will suffer.

We can see that there are many ways in which a love of nature can help us in our awareness of the angels. Silently communing with what is around us we can learn much, since nature demonstrates the angelic qualities. Mother nature shows us the rhythm of the seasons and the balance of existence. She shows us the importance of times of withdrawal in attaining peace; the necessity of acceptance—flowing with the conditions of life; the wise use of energy and play; the true freedom which comes from lack of self-consciousness and the strength which comes from being totally in the present.

Our contact with the natural world, and the balance and peace it brings, may lead us to understand better our own animal—that is, instinctive—nature, and show us how to deal wisely with our passions and fears. Love and compassion for the animals and birds is itself a route to contact with the angels, as it so obviously was for Brother Francis.

9. The Angelic Qualities of Humility and Simplicity

Besides this great love for all life, Brother Francis demonstrated the attributes of simplicity and humility; both of them qualities which open the doors to the angelic world. We may learn from Brother Francis how to contact the angels, not only through his love of the animals and birds, but also through the quality of the simplicity and humility he showed. For willingness to open to the influence of the angels also means willingness to accept God's will rather than one's own, as Brother Francis did. This is because angels bring the karmic conditions and learning and opportunities which are necessary to the soul, and from which we sometimes shrink. This is understandable because there are experiences which can cause us pain. However, in the following passages White Eagle shows us how it is often through the angels of darkness that we recognize the angels of light.

Only when the soul becomes truly humble can it be receptive to the guidance, help and love of the invisible brethren and the angelic messengers, who wait under God's command to come to you and to all people.

One of the important lessons the soul has to learn is that of humility. The wise person recognizes that all the power which comes into his or her being originates from God. Once this truth is admitted you begin to look upwards and feel the first glimmerings of light. You realize the age-old and eternal brotherhood of all living things, and then brotherhood with your own kind; and when a soul experiences this pulsation of the true brotherhood it rises into perfect happiness, light and joy. We know of no greater thrill of happiness than the feeling of the beating of the heart of a brother or a sister with our own—within our own heart.

Elsewhere White Eagle gives a moving description of the twelfth- and thirteenth-century Cathars as a group of simple brothers and sisters. In it, he demonstrates the great power and inner vision—the ability to live with and contact the angels—which comes with the attribute of humility:

The Brotherhood known as the Albigenses [Cathars] was a brotherhood of sweetness and simplicity. They were very simple brothers and sisters. They lived a communal life, and they lived to serve all creatures. They received from the one you know as St John the secret of developing those spiritual senses which enabled them to see clairvoyantly the spirit land and the spirit life. The Albigenses lived so close to God and to nature and to all the angels. Even when they were walled up in the cave they held hands and they were all in a state of ecstasy. They went forth into the world of spirit in full consciousness, seeing the angels waiting there to receive them. And what have you to do in order to qualify for this experience? You have to live a simple, brotherly life, pure and whole, human, angelic; just dear sweet souls.

What we see from this is that true humility is not a weak feeling of being less than others, but rather, a strong inner belief and trust in

God, so that the outer self can let go. With this trust in the power of the spirit in our lives there is no need to fight or defend. We can be what we are, unique and simple children of God. Trust in the rightness of the divine plan and divine laws brings a sense of freedom. It brings freedom from anxiety, possessiveness and the persistent thoughts we have which cloud our inner vision.

However, to let go and to trust is not easy. Our very being in matter leads to a feeling of separation from God and from each other, which at times may cause us to feel that life is a lesson in surviving, and may cause us to hold on tightly to all that makes us feel secure. But White Eagle speaks often of how fears and anxieties get in the way of our realizing our true nature. He tells us that there is no need to fear, no need for the anxieties which tend to dominate our daily lives: fears of not fitting in, of being seen as simple, of disdain from our peers, of not being lovable or lovely. Instead he reminds us how much we are unconditionally loved and cared for.

How then do we help ourselves to stay open to the angels' presence, to be simple, and to have that trust in the spirit which comes from knowing we are loved? How do we retain that trust so that we can be truly accepting and give our hearts full play, in order to be more receptive to 'seeing' and feeling the angels' presence?

Trusting in the presence of the spirit, we can be as simple as the Albigenses, and thus command the power they had to walk into death singing, as White Eagle describes. Often this trust can be encouraged through acts of spontaneity and creativity—like the play of a child. It is especially true of dancing, singing, running or laughing, or of playing the drums or any other musical instrument in an uninhibited way. Any activity of mind or body which breaks down rigidity encourages trust. This kind of movement can bring a feeling of liberation from restriction—the spontaneity and lack of structure in it allows plenty of opportunity for the controlling mind to be put in abeyance, and for the joy of the intuition and spirit to flood in.

It is interesting how many religious groups have some sort of dancing or singing as part of their worship. White Eagle has often talked about how Jesus loved to dance, and was filled with spontaneous joy—that joy which sets a child's feet leaping and spinning with the wind and by the sea. Encouraging ourselves to be uninhibited is one way to develop the trust we need: trust in our bodies, the uniqueness of our creativity, and our inner expression, and therefore trust in the spirit which upholds us all. What is more, the fairy folk love to dance, and the angels are called by music and any creative form of expression. There is a wonderful lightness of being, and feeling of rightness which comes from letting go of rigidity and uptightness; an ability to flow with how things are, rather than a need to control.

The spiritual teaching of Taoism stresses this importance of flowing with the Tao—with what is. In his book THE TAO OF LEADERSHIP—an adaptation of the classic ancient Chinese text, the *Tao Te Ching* by Lao Tzu—John Heider has paraphrased the text thus:

'From knowing how things work, I also know the importance of staying flexible. Everything that grows is flexible. All enduring strength is flexible....

'Consider the lives of plants and trees: during their time of greatest growth, they are relatively tender and pliant.'*

Whatever our age, physical circumstances or fitness, we can flow with life rather than try to resist it. However, this does not mean being pulled hither and thither—a dancer, and a bird, know how much need there is for balance in order to be able to fly! 'Being centred means having the ability to recover one's balance, even in the midst of action.'†

Life itself has a way of helping us develop this quality of flexibility, for nothing is fixed and rigid in the natural world. Physical life is a process of constant change, and even at the equator there are seasonal features in the weather patterns. To live with change and em-

* *London (Wildwood House), 1986, pp. 103, 151* †*p. 51*

brace it in a positive way is one of the challenges of being human, and what we can discover when we let go is the divine spirit—which is always there for us, and which is our ground and stability in the midst of all life's changes. We may fear to lose our sense of self, even our integrity, when we are flexible; but in fact it makes us strong. Acts of thankfulness and forgiveness, for example, bring us back to the sweetness of our undefended self. Telling someone how grateful we are, or apologizing when we make mistakes, loosens our defences, and in so doing puts us back in touch with the strength of our true spirit within.

What is it we love about an animal or a very young child? It could be a response to their vulnerability, and their openness of expression. When we too demonstrate—through our gratitude, and our willingness to apologize and to be seen to be imperfect—this same vulnerability, we give those around us a glimpse into our heart. We allow them into the place in each one of us which is unique, but where magically we are linked in spirit with each other, and with the angels.

An important part of the humility we may be seeking is to be prepared to acknowledge and embrace our innocence and simplicity, our meekness and our weaknesses, without guilt or shame. We might feel ashamed to allow the world to see our imperfections, we might be fearful of derision, pity or dislike. But actually people are relieved by openness, and cycles of mistrust are broken by it. John Heider's paraphrase of the *Tao Te Ching* gives us further relevant insights into human nature.

'Why is the ocean the greatest body of water? Because it lies below all the rivers and streams and is open to them all....

'The wise leader knows that yielding overcomes resistances, and gentleness melts rigid defences.... If the leader were not like water, the leader would break. The ability to be soft makes the leader a leader.... This is another paradox: what is soft is strong.'*

*pp. 131, 155

What I feel White Eagle and the Tao tell us is that when we are vulnerable we need not feel shame, for we are giving a priceless gift to another, and showing that we believe in a strength within which is beyond the defensiveness of the earth. 'Meekness is not weakness', he says. It is the same strength which enabled the master Jesus to bear the crown of thorns, the jeering and the mocking; which enabled him to say *O my Father, if it be possible, let this cup pass from me: nevertheless, not as I will, but as thou wilt,* and thereby to release into the world the majesty and power of the Christ light reborn.

White Eagle refers to this ultimate sacrifice of all that the self holds dear as the earth initiation (something which you can read more about in his book THE PATH OF THE SOUL). It is an experience which we all go through many times in a minor way, and if we are open to them the angels of the earth element will always be drawn to us at such a time. Often, those who are experiencing the earth initiation have a deep love of the natural world, as did Francis of Assisi. What comes across to us as his self-sacrifice, his simple-heartedness, is the very quality which drew the animals to him. This also put him in touch with the angelic consciousness in such a profound way that he could enter their world and communicate with all the life of the earth.

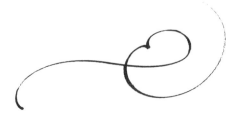

10. The Angelic Qualities of Harmony and Beauty

The natural world gives us countless visions and experiences of the angelic qualities of harmony and beauty. Angels are attracted to beauty because they are beautiful themselves. They are beautiful in the way in which they represent perfect harmony. They live in a state of balance: nothing jars in what they are or do, because all is appropriate, pure and true to the divine purpose which they serve. White Eagle links beauty and harmony together in this way:

> Many of you will know that from time to time we have spoken on the need for harmony. This can be misunderstood. By 'living in harmony' we do not mean being unaware of things which need to be righted. By harmony we mean training the self to do everything that seems to be necessary in the most beautiful way—not necessarily the easy way, but the beautiful way.
>
> As you begin to become aware of what is taking place inside you; as you live with your eyes open so that you see always beauty and never destruction; as you begin to see with the eyes of your spirit the beauty in nature and within all the elements, you become attuned to the creative spheres. As you perhaps start to follow your soul's urge towards some

creative art, angels from those creative spheres are drawn to you; they watch your work and inspire and guide you.

The recognition of beauty which the angels foster in us can be a recognition of beauty in the most outwardly ugly of situations. In fact they bring an ability to see beauty where others may not. If you can begin to be aware of, and have faith in, the greater plan—a plan which involves more than the transient, illusory pleasures of the earth plane—then you are not merely captivated by the beauty experienced by the earthly senses, but becoming aware of a loveliness which is deeper than this. It is a beauty based on the 'rightness' of God's laws, and the outworking of the Christ light in all beings, things and conditions. An analogy of this in the creative arts is a piece of music in which apparently intense discords can bring a far greater beauty to the whole work than a sequence of immediately 'pleasant' sounds. Perhaps this is a helpful way of looking at difficulties in ourselves and our everyday lives!

> You must train yourself to behold beauty in many forms. See the beauty in the light of another's face, the beauty of love in the eyes of a child, the beauty of love and light in the eyes and in the face of a very old person. Look always for that light, that beauty. Beautiful form is a manifestation of God and all Godlike qualities. But until that beauty has a correspondence in the beholder it does not exist. Within *you* lies the beauty and the power to behold and also to manifest beauty.

Thus, when we see beauty in places and people and events which are not obviously beautiful in the eyes of material humanity, we are helping the angels to bring harmony and balance there to an even greater degree. Whenever we see beauty in this way, we are in touch with angels. You know how, when something strikes you as lovely, a feeling stirs in your heart? A lightness comes—and this is the touch of the angels.

> Beauty is always a manifestation of God's harmonies to humanity. When you walk in the fields and in the lanes you can see this manifestation in every flower; indeed, in every blade of grass and in each bush and tree. Even then, only a part of the beauty of God can be seen, and even to this many people are blind. So it is well to cultivate the power of observation. Only when you are quiet in spirit do you have time to observe the shining loveliness of the dew on grass and flower, the delicate colourings of wild flowers and the sheen of sunlight through the trees. As you unfold you will be able to observe the nature spirits at work in grass and flower, bush and tree, and walk in companionship with water, wind and sunlight. You will then enter what the children call the fairy world.

How then do we train ourselves to be aware of beauty? What do we do with the vision of disharmony and unpleasantness? The secret lies in the way in which White Eagle links beauty with harmony. He tells us to create harmony by doing things in the most beautiful way. The converse is also true: we can be creators of beauty wherever we are, by bringing harmony and balance into what we see and experience.

When we appreciate a wonderful painting, or look at a lovely natural scene, the beauty in it is often created by the juxtaposition of light and darkness, movement and stillness, impressions of sound and of silence. There is an inherent harmony which is created by the balancing of seeming opposites. When we are aware of ugliness and distress, what more beautiful thing can we do than to surround and balance that discord with its opposite—with light and healing thoughts?

We can thus be co-creators with God, not only through our creative arts, which White Eagle talks about in the next chapter, but through our ability to balance anything which seems evil with the goodness of our thoughts and aspirations. You may have noticed how very often good things do come out of seemingly negative events, and this is because it is a law of the universe—a divine law—that there should always be balance between darkness and light. The angels of darkness and light are in perfect balance; the masters and workers on the inner planes, along with the angels, keep the balance on the earth plane, so that besides learning through pain and suffering, humanity will also grow in light, and blossom.

If we transform an inharmonious and ugly situation into one of beauty and peace—either through what we do or, more importantly, through the power and light of our loving thoughts—then we are joining with the forces which keep the whole of creation on track. We link with the angels of darkness and light in the creation of harmony.

When we do this, we work under the seventh ray—what White Eagle calls 'the ray of beauty'. If you read the account of this ray on page 104, you will see how White Eagle links this ray with those who love beauty, colour and harmony, and how this love brings the angels of ceremonial very close, because in any ceremony there are powers intensified by the love of beauty. Therefore, another way in which we can develop beauty within and around ourselves, and thus bring the angels closer, is to create and take part in harmonious ceremonies and rituals. This does not necessarily mean only great or communal events, for harmonious rituals can also be created around daily or weekly events in one's ordinary life.

We can make a harmonious, thoughtful ritual out of our daily quiet time just by the considered and quiet way we light a candle or arrange the room. Even more than this, we can bring the feeling of beauty into all the activities of life through the harmonious way in which we approach them. Ceremony and ritual, in order to have power and meaning, need to be carried out in particular ways: there has to be a mindfulness of what we are doing, a peaceful and measured pace to our actions; a gentleness of approach, but with a clear and uncluttered vision of the appropriate action. There needs to be a sense of the rightness and point of each moment.

You can see from this that we can apply all these qualities to what we do in daily life. White Eagle talks about doing things one at a time and in an unhurried way, and of having one's whole attention on the job in hand. This too is bringing into daily life the power of ceremony, so that in all of life there is the opportunity for creating beauty and harmony.

Often White Eagle is teaching us about an inner approach to life more than about what we do outwardly. So while you may not appear, on the outside, to be doing anything different, inwardly you may be allowing the qualities of ritual and ceremony to influence your actions and speech. This does not mean that you begin to talk in an accented and holy voice, or move around like a priest! To do that in your office, neighbourhood or home would be inharmonious in itself! In fact it means that you would more readily see the *appropriate and most harmonious* way of being in any situation and respond accordingly. The angels will help—they will be drawn to your aspiration.*

Harmony is an angelic quality which can be fostered by balancing our lives and our energy. We feel out of kilter when, through our hurt and fear, the pendulum of the self is stuck in one or another extreme of thought, feeling or reaction; or when it swings wildly between them. One simple thing that helps is to notice is whether in your life there is a fair balance between mental, physical, emotional

* *White Eagle's teaching on the angels of ritual and ceremonial forms chapter 21 of this book.*

and spiritual pursuits. Is there balance between play and work; creativity and receptivity? During the course of a day, or even a week, it may not be possible to keep such a balance, but over a month and the whole year it may be. Times of work and mental activity during the week can be balanced by active and emotional pursuits at the weekend. Some people who have a strong mind in this incarnation may need to balance it with more opportunities for creativity and play, for example. In this way you are helping to balance the four elements and bring harmony to the whole being.

I feel that another way to increase a sense of harmony within is to be mindful whenever we show extremes of emotion or thought. Very strongly-held opinions, or violent likes and dislikes, are an extreme reaction to life. A habitually strong negative emotion is like a discordant note struck on the inner planes of our being and in our aura, which creates disharmony.

However, I do believe that it will not help to condemn ourselves for this, because for some of us this is the lesson of life: learning to balance and harmonize, and possibly release the need for that strong negative feeling. This applies whether the feeling is fear or anger or guilt. For others the lesson is to transcend or transform the powerful mental pull of criticism, or bigotry. All we can expect of ourselves is the aspiration to do this, and the angels will draw close to those who sincerely attempt to bring harmony to their being in this way.

What I feel we must remember is that we have chosen to deal with these so-called negative feelings and thoughts because we are truly seeking to bring harmony to the soul. There is, in fact, a *harmonious* reason for us having them in the first place. We simply are not inherently sinful or failures, even when the harmonious way eludes us for our whole life. White Eagle reminds us that we cannot know what is the true need of the soul, nor are we often aware of how *much* we are succeeding. Mastership may elude us for many, many lives to come! So the best way to live with your imperfect self is to live in

harmony with yourself as a whole; to be gentle, tolerant and understanding of yourself and your apparent failings; to be wise in your
thoughts about yourself. Not harsh, punitive or over-strict, but patient and accepting of the limitations of earth.

So how, if we are struggling with mental or emotional control, do
we bring harmony into this struggle? How can we find any sort of
balance while the emotions are still strong? I believe that what lies at
the heart of White Eagle's teaching—indeed at the heart of any true
spiritual teaching—and the first step in any spiritual development, is
the knowledge that we are loved, unconditionally and without end.
This awareness of being loved, even when we are struggling for mental
and emotional control, is what brings harmony. It is this balance
which prevents us plunging into despair, or giving up entirely. More
than this, our faith in the unconditional love which embraces us is
what will eventually enable us to be free, joyous, and fearless, and is
what enables us truly to love under all circumstances.

Just for a moment, imagine the veil between you and the next
world falling away completely. What would you see? What would
you feel and experience? No matter what is happening in your life,
right now as you read this, and without closing your eyes, just think
of there being no limit to your vision, no veil between this state of
consciousness you are in and the inner state. What I believe you would
immediately be aware of is that you are utterly and completely loved.
This love fills your mind and your emotions like autumn rains rushing to fill a river bed, dry and parched from heat. You are conscious
that everything about you is known with the greatest possible understanding. All your fears and failings, your longings and needs, are
known in a way which makes you feel safe and at the same time not
at all stupid for having those emotions; all your feelings of loss or
unrequited need are understood. This love rushes in to fill the hol-
low, dry spaces inside; it brings you wondrous recompense for your
sorrow. It brings you the almost incredible awareness that nothing

and no-one is ever lost to you; that nothing you have ever longed for is denied. This love makes you feel young and vital—alive and creative and full of energy—and at the same time so nurtured that you feel the deepest comfort and peace. This love reawakens in you longed-for feelings of hope and faith, of belief in goodness and kindness and a greater plan—in a gentler world. Looking around you at the earthly level all becomes beautiful, even in its imperfection, because of this belief and the trust which love engenders.

This is the love of God—of the Great Spirit—the love which the angels serve. Know that you are loved; seek to know this, imagine this, think this, feel this, if only for a moment, and all else will follow. You will know what to do and how to be, for love breeds love, and it calls to the love within you to arise and shine like a star.

Your own spiritual teacher and guide knows every aspiration and every difficulty that you endure, and that guide loves you more than you can love yourself. He or she is with you to help you in every possible way. You are comrades, and the guide often smoothes your path.... Although the law of karma is exact, just, perfect and true, remember that God is a God of mercy as well as justice, and has a way, through all the ministers of light, of smoothing the rough corners. God's love blesses and helps you.

White Eagle, SPIRITUAL UNFOLDMENT I

11. Responding to the Creative Stream

It is because of the angels' work and presence that beautiful creations come into being. For we can see, from what White Eagle has
already said, that it is through beauty that we touch the creative
spheres: 'As you begin to see with the eyes of your spirit the beauty in
nature and within all the elements, you become attuned to the creative spheres.'

Angels are God's messengers and channels for the creative energy of the universe to be poured upon the earth and into the hearts
and minds of people. Therefore an appreciation of beauty, no matter where we find it, itself opens up a channel to those angelic
messengers, and allows them to help and inspire us even further.
It may sound very grand to say this, but White Eagle has assured us
that when we work in our own way with the angels through an appreciation of beauty and harmony, we become co-creators with
God. We help the angels to beautify and thus harmonize the whole
planet.

When we are creative in any way, or when we use our imagination or our senses of appreciation and harmony, we are drawing
angels to us. Angels are messengers of creation and of growth
and so all the creative arts are directly influenced by them, as are all
the ways in which we receive inspiration, new ideas and awareness.

They influence our 'becoming', and the 'becoming' of the whole universe. A new idea, a new juxtaposition of colour or form, a seemingly accidental creation: each of these, we can be sure, has been influenced in some way by the angels, even though we may not be conscious of how this has taken place. For example, White Eagle has talked frequently about the influence of the angels of music:

> Angels of music draw close to those who call on them. When you know how to call on these angelic beings they can pour into you creative power, which enables you to express more readily the music of your soul. So also with literature and painting, or with any of the creative arts. No words can describe the angels which come when there is beautiful music to be heard. They are taking the substance, the colour and the form which is being created by the sounds, and weaving it into indescribably lovely forms.
>
> The seven notes of music create, by their vibration, seven colour rays. Next time you go to an orchestral concert and feel the vibrations of the music stirring your soul, let your imagination run riot and imagine the colours which certain themes produce. Never mind if you make a mistake. You can interpret all harmonies by the different degrees of colour. Remember what we have said about the varying shades of each colour, and their interpenetration: even with music, do not think exclusively of one colour. There is a predominant shade, but also many variations. The vibrations, the harmony of music, strike a certain centre in the soul, and cause it to open like a flower—to the sunlight, to the white light of the Son, of the Christ, expressed by harmony.
>
> Each composer has a special work to do. His or her music comes from the inner planes and is intended to produce

certain effects upon the physical and subtle bodies of the people who listen. Thus different musicians introduce a certain quality which humanity especially needed at the time it was brought through, and also during the course of the evolution of the race. The composer receives these creations from great devas, from great angels: those who are responsible for the creation or recreation of artistic, music and spiritual life in the people of earth.

The following passage of White Eagle's teaching was given during a time of meditation in a service. As we read it our limited consciousness expands to perceive something of the harmony of the creative spheres in the spiritual life:

We take you now into the world of spirit, into the great temple of music. You yourself must open your inner vision and see *your* temple of music ... see it ... hear it ... feel it.... See the beautiful structure, the pulsating colour of the pillars and the canopy overhead. Notice the iridescent colours in the very substance of the temple. See the colour proceeding from those wonderful, heavenly stringed instruments, and other instruments of music unknown to your earth. Listen to this heavenly harmony, which begins gently and quietly, describing all the aspects of nature and the work of the nature spirits, the running water and the gentle breeze, the perfume of the flowers ... God everywhere being expressed in beauty, sound and perfume.... Hear the power and the richness of the drums ... can you feel the vibration of this music? And then the gentle, sweet stringed instruments. And when you hear the wind instruments you see the forces of the air, the air devas, cleansing. Feel you are within the forces of nature in this spirit temple of music. Here the musicians learn the laws of sound and the action of sound on etheric and physical matter.

Your souls are attuned to this heavenly orchestra, and you can hear the great *Aum … Aum.…* The vibration ripples on and on and on, in ever-widening circles … wider and wider, right out into outer space. You are taken with the sound and are in it.… Feel the beneficent, tender love which comes to the souls of men and women on earth in that sweet and gentle sound; the heavenly music which opens the soul to the love of God. When you listen to your music on earth, let it do for you what we are trying to convey to you tonight.

It is listening with the whole being that really brings about contact with the angels of music: imagining the colours they bring, feeling the forces of nature that are expressed. On many occasions White Eagle has told us the secret of how to listen to something deeper than earthly sound through listening in the natural world. The following passage comes from his book THE GENTLE BROTHER:

You want to listen to the spirit world, to listen to the words of love spoken by your beloved in the beyond, by your guide, your teacher, and later by your master? Learn then to listen first to people on the earth, to give your whole attention to the one who is speaking to you; listen also to the sounds of the birds and animals, the song of the wind in the trees, of the falling raindrops and the rushing river. This is how the Native Americans were trained from childhood; and because they were so trained, they were able to hear not only physical sounds, but sounds behind those of earth, the sounds of the unseen world. They could distinguish the voices of their spirit guides and teachers; they could also hear the nature spirits.

One of the limitations we set ourselves when faced with creative opportunities is lack of confidence. There is huge pressure on us to compare ourselves with others, and to deny our ability to be open to this creative stream. 'Why me?' is the question most asked; but then, why not me? As Nelson Mandela has said in a famous speech: 'We are born to make manifest the glory of God that is within us; it's not just in some of us, it's in everyone'. Perhaps not everyone can be a Beethoven or a Mozart at the moment, but for each of us there is that link with the creative spheres, and the opportunity, with devotion, commitment, and (it has to be said) sometimes much application, to create beauty.

To be confident means deeply acknowledging our birthright as a son or daughter of God; as a spiritual being. Far from making us egotistical, that awareness of being 'spirit first' as White Eagle puts it, actually enables us to let go more, and be more open to other spiritual beings—both on earth and in heaven. We are not seeking then to hold everything to ourselves, but we are inwardly strong enough to give and to share. It is through being able to give and to share that we can create; the angels draw close to those who truly seek to give, and in giving and creating we ourselves in turn receive. So it is that the world and all beings grow together in spiritual consciousness.

Our growing confidence in being able to be open to the angels itself increases our receptivity to their help. Confidence is a matter of faith—first belief, and then faith, that the angels can truly be drawn to us; since no matter what the earthly self may seem to be, we are sparks of the divine. Letting go a sense of restriction within, letting go the sense of being only human, allows the angels greater access to our consciousness, and through them we can be inspired and guided.

Appreciation and gratitude for the harmony and beauty which surrounds us enables us to be open to this creative stream. So too we will more readily be attuned to the angels of creativity if we have in our hearts the wish to bring more of this beauty into manifestation on earth for the joy it can bring to others.

White Eagle says:

Remember always that you are working on the inner planes with these powerful but invisible forces; and that your thought, your speech, and your emotion are all used by those forces. But you are the arbiter. It is in *you*. The power lies in *you*, and you have it in your power, by your devotion to and love of God and His–Her angelic servers, to heal the wounds of humanity and to bring heavenly light and understanding, heavenly comfort and peace, into the mind and the heart of human kind.

INTERLUDE
Working with the Angels—White Eagle's
Prayer for Humanity

One of the key aspects of service which White Eagle has offered us is to call upon the angels of Christ through active prayer. He has suggested words to use, but the prayer always consists in using the creative imagination to send out the light to humanity, and especially to those people who suffer, to the animal kingdom, and to the earth herself.

Anyone can offer themselves in service in this way. Indeed, anyone who becomes a member of the Lodge, or feels in harmony with White Eagle's teaching, is invited to join in this healing work, especially at the hours each day of 3.00, 6.00, 9.00, and 12.00, a.m. and p.m., or at least at any of those hours for which we may be awake and able to participate. At these times, White Eagle says, we are better able to raise our consciousness to the spheres of light. So too, as a result of people in countries all over the world joining in this directed prayer at the same time, there is an increase in the power of the projection, and a constant stream of loving, healing thought goes forth. White Eagle says:

> Always more power is created in a group. There are some
> who feel that they can do better work alone, because they

do not like the conditions or the vibrations of other people, but you see, my dear ones, if you can get above the weakness of the human self, which tends to be exclusive, and rise into that infinite love, then you can become part of a far greater power than if you were working on your own.

In the new age, the age of Aquarius, the age of the spirit, you will find more and more that humanity will gather into groups for their work, because a greater power is generated in this way. In this absent healing work all time and space is overcome. You go up into that higher consciousness, into the life of the spiritual Son, of Christ, and it is from that source that you work. You make contact with the Christ sphere, the Christ circle, and in that Christ circle are the angels. The six-pointed star, which pulsates with the healing power, is a magnet which draws the angels. At the command of the Lord of creation they wing their way; they wing their way in service to the sick and the sad; to bereaved and sorrowful humanity; and they illumine the consciousness of human kind.

It is then like an ocean; wave upon wave upon wave of this creative healing power is continually going forth. But so wonderful is the spiritual law that the human contact, through willing hearts on earth, is necessary before the angels can make contact at the physical level of life.

Overleaf is the full text of White Eagle's Prayer for Humanity. This is used in all services in the White Eagle Lodge throughout the world, and an adaptation of it is used at noon each day in the major centres.

There is a shorter version of the same prayer which can be used on a daily basis, at the magical hours, and this is given beneath the main prayer overleaf. During the working day, whether in office, shop,

WHITE EAGLE'S PRAYER FOR ALL HUMANITY

Let us remember before God the need of all human kind; and that we may pray to God, we make quiet the fretful mind of every day.... Let us open our hearts to the Father–Mother God and to Christ the Son ... to the holy trinity of wisdom ... love ... and power.

In the holy name of Christ; by the Christ light in the hearts of all people, we call upon the great angels of Christ. We feel their presence and their power. We attune ourselves to the prayers of all men and women of goodwill.

Being thus prepared, and ready before God, with all the will of our minds, and with all the love of our deepest hearts, we send forth the light. We send it forth as a great star of light ... a blazing star ... withstanding, overcoming all evil; triumphant over darkness and death ... a star of the Christ light.

By all the power of Christ within our hearts, we send forth the light. Amen.

SHORTER VERSION

We hold all humanity in the golden light of the Christ Star, and see the power of the Son of God working in the hearts of all people....

We behold the blazing star, with the form of the Lord Christ within its centre, radiating his beauty, his spirit, his love over all the earth.

We hold all who have asked for help or healing within this golden healing light.

At this point, if there is anyone known to you personally who is in need of help or healing, silently name them, and see them perfect in the heart of the star.

May God's blessing be upon this work. Amen.

factory or home, one can simply tune in, with or without words, in the powerful silence of the heart. For just a few moments one can visualize the light of the blazing six-pointed star radiating out over the earth, bringing peace and healing to humanity.* The use of 'we' in the prayer is deliberate—for one does not work alone, but companioned by angels.

In the passage of teaching on pp. 86–87, White Eagle is particularly referring to the absent healing work of the Lodge, where a group of six committed healers sit regularly to send out the light to specific patients. However, in all the healing work in the Lodge, from the first time one uses the Prayer for Humanity, through the absent and lone healing work, to the service of contact healing, there is this emphasis on deliberately calling on the angels of healing—'messengers of the spirit; the sons of the flame', as White Eagle has called them—in order to work in harmony with them and thus with divine law.†

*For those who are unfamiliar with the work of the White Eagle Lodge, the significance of the six-pointed star will become clearer on reading chapter 13, about the seven rays, in the second part of this book. It is like seeing and helping to bring into manifestation the perfect spirit within the person or condition in need of healing.

†More is said specifically about the angels of healing in the second part of this book.

PART TWO

12. Introduction: the Angelic Stream of Life

So far we have been looking at some of the angelic qualities—the soul qualities which, White Eagle says, are made manifest by the angels; those we can aspire to develop in ourselves, to help us vibrate harmoniously with the angelic consciousness. White Eagle has shown us how the motives which underlie our aspiration need to be loving and brotherly, and to come from a sense of oneness with all life.

I hope that the following chapters will enhance your own awareness of this interrelation. Maybe you will experience something of the same wonder and sense of belonging a friend of mine felt when reading the teaching contained in them. She found through becoming a little more aware of the vast plan for all life (not just in this age and solar system, but throughout space and time) and of the part the angelic hierarchy play in this plan, that her own difficulties and suffering had more meaning, and at the same time less heaviness. As she read, she found that the boundaries which are part of physical life just disappeared; and the feeling which came was that if she could experience this through White Eagle's words, however fleetingly, then she must have that eternal self within.

As you read White Eagle's descriptions, you may experience your own unique sense of connection; or may catch a glimpse of the immensity and exactness of God's universe and our relation to it.

I think, however, that we may only understand a little of this plan, for to comprehend all would be beyond the mortal mind to absorb. Because of this, I have begun this part of the book with some of White Eagle's words about the nature of truth and the mystery of life. Here he conveys to us the importance of an open heart, and a mind which is not too rigid in its conception of things, for there is much that he cannot begin to explain to us of the magic of God's creation and plan, and the work of the angels.

In spiritual life, do not expect to catalogue everything, for by so doing you are limiting the universal. Try to conceive the heavenly state as being a perfect fitting-in and harmonious outworking of exact law, but never limited, always expanding. We do not like to make things too set, so that a sense of limitation comes over, or a closed-in comprehension of the truth. Remember that you enter infinity when you are in the world of spirit.

When it proves beyond speech to describe cosmic truth, there is only one way left for the aspirant to learn; and that is through leaving the physical consciousness and rising into the heavens, and through seeing for him or herself. This is why we do not care for any sort of crossing of the t's and dotting of the i's. We do not like cataloguing and pigeonholing cosmic truth. That is what the intellect strives after, but spiritual truth always escapes the grasp of the intellect. It remains for every aspirant to rise through those planes of consciousness to know, within the soul, truths which cannot be clothed in words, which cannot be catalogued.

13. Rays from the Spiritual Sun

Fully to appreciate the incredible power and the extent of the plan of the spirit is, as White Eagle has said, impossible for the finite mind. Nevertheless, he helps us towards an idea of it in the following passages. It is good to read them with the mind open to the intuition, and with an awareness of the interpenetration and oneness of life. White Eagle's intention, as he has said, is not so much to spell out all the details, but to give a picture of the grandeur of life. Quoting again from the beginning of St John's gospel, he says:

In the beginning was the Word, and the Word was with God, and the Word was God. In the beginning was light; all things are formed through *light*. If there were no light at all on earth, if there were total darkness, there would be no life. Light is sometimes called the 'Son' of God. The *Son* means the spiritual Sun; a spiritual sunlight existing within, behind and all around the sun. As the physical sun's rays continually pour down on the earth, bestowing life and light and creating harmony in nature, harmony in the spheres, so the spiritual Sun gives life and light to the human soul.

For light is a power, a substance, contained within the earth. It is absorbed and drawn up, and then reflected again onto the earth. The cosmic rays from the heart of the spiritual Sun are not exactly light, but they have the power to operate a force which will create light.

Think of the first great cause, which perhaps it is easiest for you to conceive as the blazing, eternal spiritual Sun. Conceive within this Sun the triangle (symbolizing the trinity of many religions). These are the three who have always been since the beginning; who are concerned purely with the solar system and the evolution of the earth planet, and who are best understood as the three aspects, wisdom, love and power. These are the three from whom all life comes. From this trinity of wisdom, love and power comes also the angelic line of service, concerned with life in form throughout every kingdom.

Think again of the great cause, the Sun. See, now, from the Sun, the seven rays, the seven colours of the spectrum; the seven notes of music—for each note of music represents a colour and a cosmic ray—see the rays from the Sun, or this 'first principle', permeating all life and the whole universe. Each ray is connected with the Sun and all the angels of the rays work in the souls of people for the evolution, the growth and the gradual perfecting of the individual.

There are seven rays, and seven great beings, referred to in the bible as 'the seven angels round the throne', who are called the Elohim, or the seven silent watchers at the head of their own particular ray. These rays are used to stimulate or assist humanity in its upward climb back to the central Sun, to the centre of life.

Before describing the attributes of the seven rays (the list overleaf is constructed from his original talk) White Eagle deliberately stressed that there would be many such attempts to put what is an enormous

Ray	White Eagle's Notes	Colour	Note
1. POWER	'The first ray is the ray of Will. It is the lawgiver, the ruler.'	Red	Do
2. LOVE	'The second ray we will call the ray of Philanthropy—some call it the altruistic ray. Those who vibrate to this are people who are working always under the influence of love. The first ray was Power, and now Love; you will notice that with the third we form our triangle.'	Orange	Re
3. WISDOM	'The third ray is very beautiful. Shall we call it the ray of Philosophy, the ray of the thinker?'	Yellow	Mi
4. HARMONY	'The fourth ray we will call the ray of Harmony; an expression in form of higher things.'	Green	Fa
5. WISDOM	'The fifth ray is the ray of Science. By this we mean also religious science—the science of prayer. Another wisdom ray.'	Blue	So
6. LOVE	'The sixth ray is another ray of Love, the ray of true goodness. The ray of the mystic.'	Indigo	La
7. POWER	'The seventh ray is the ray of Beauty. It brings into operation those powers which are intensified by beauty, and draws to its influence or surroundings those great devas which are present at ceremonies. In this way the seventh ray is interpreted by some as the ceremonial ray. We will call it however, the ray of Beauty, being an aspect of God.'	Violet	Ti

and magnificent spiritual organization into words. It is worth mentioning that he deliberately stressed that all such attempts would be slightly different because of the difficulty of limiting such a vast panorama in the restricted language and understanding of the earth plane.

Here is another example of how White Eagle tries to enlarge our limited understanding of these angelic beings:

It is impossible to describe their radiance. The unskilled artist may daub a canvas with colour and convey nothing of the beauty of the original. Could you describe the perfume of the flower? The perfume is beyond words.

These beings from the solar sphere are concerned with the masses of humanity. They are concerned with the quickening of the light of the Son in the heart, and concerned with the ushering-in of great ages or epochs.

Between you and the heavens above are angels, continually working in every form of life on earth to bring sustenance, to bring health, to assist growth and development. Few realize the grandeur and the extent of the heavenly hosts concerned with life on the earth plane.

Joan Hodgson adds (in PLANETARY HARMONIES, p. 29):

'The Lords of the seven rays which pour forth from the spiritual Sun are sometimes known as the sons of the flame, or as the angels round the throne of God. From these seven rays all creation comes into being. All mineral, plant, animal or human life is permeated by these planetary forces. In the mineral kingdom this penetration is a latent force awaiting development, but it gives the metal, stone or jewel its own special vibration. In plant life the quickening ray of the planet manifests in more complex form. In the animal kingdom there comes a blending of planetary influences; while at the human stage the soul represents a universe in miniature, which the ray of the Sun links directly with the solar logos [i.e., the Word]. All the planetary rays playing upon that soul intermingle to produce the myriad variations in physical, mental and psychic characteristics. The spirit in humanity, the Christ within, has so to rule its own universe that all the elements harmoniously combine to produce the perfect Sun-man or Sun-woman.

'The whole solar universe is so marvellously governed, the planetary angels so perfectly organized, each in his or her own sphere, that the tiniest detail of life is within the divine, immutable law.'

White Eagle says: 'Try to get a broad vision, and remember that there are other systems, other suns, other universes, and yet all are linked and are all part of the one great whole'. He was once asked: 'Can you tell us a geometric figure that would express seven rays?' And he replied:

Let us take the triangle on its base, and also the triangle on its apex; then, putting them together, right in the centre of the star shines the middle ray, the ray of Harmony. Visualize the six-pointed star with the seventh point in its centre, and see there the great companies, the hierarchies of those seven points of the magic star.

All life is interconnected, and a human being mirrors in him or herself the macrocosm. Indeed, White Eagle has said that we are made up of countless millions of six-pointed stars! Thus all the colours, with their corresponding notes and perfumes, are within ourselves, and on various different levels, tones or octaves, according to what degree of soul quality we are working on in this lifetime. White Eagle has told us that until we reach a certain stage of being able to get above the passions and strife of human life, we are partly influenced by all the rays, and may not vibrate to any particular one. In the end it is a question of attaining perfect balance between all the rays, within the soul (not perhaps in the limited personality of one incarnation), and it is interesting that White Eagle has placed the ray of harmony and balance at the central point of the six-pointed star.

Attunement to the Seven Rays

The following passages are not necessarily intended to be read straight through as a whole, but are contemplations on each of the divine rays, drawing on White Eagle's teaching. They can be used to help us understand ways of 'earthing' the energies of the rays more in the human personality and forms of earth. White Eagle has always sought to help us realize the divine in the human, and to raise our consciousness in meditation in order to spiritualize matter, rather than escape from it. In this way our own meditations become more than just experiences for our own spiritual growth. Each contact with the spirit that we make while in a physical body benefits the whole world.

I suggest the following as a picture of this: imagine that the whole world and all its people are inside a giant egg, with a spiritual light outside that is beautiful almost beyond comprehension and yet only dimly seen through the screen made by the shell. Each person is given a hammer, which they can use, if they wish, to chip away at the bit of shell in front of them. As each does this, they make little cracks and tiny holes, through which the bright light reaches into the whole egg. It reaches not just that part of the egg where the person stands, but everywhere. All benefit from one person's activity.

A meditation on the first ray

As we seek to attune ourselves to the angels of the first ray, the ray of will, it must be remembered that the will to which we are attuning ourselves is ultimately divine will—although White Eagle has told us that human will is also necessary to give us the courage and the endurance to proceed. However, the most important inner statement we can make when we put ourselves under the red ray is still 'thy will be done'. With this inner acceptance of divine will and the divine plan for life, we can safely and with humility call upon the strength and determination of these angels.

In meditation you might find yourself at the heart of a great temple, where there is a flame of intense power reaching from the floor up through the roof and on into the centre of the Sun. When you stand at the centre of that flame, what comes is a feeling of awe, and with it intense devotion as you become aware in a small degree of the enormous spiritual force which governs all life. At that moment all self-will is stripped away in the cleansing fire, and you are filled with 'the will to will the will of God'. This is what brings true power, and is the true purpose of this ray on its highest octave. When you leave that temple you are renewed in courage and fortitude, and with a renewed awareness of what it means to be a child of that Great Spirit—the responsibility and the joy! For the angels of the first ray bring the joy of the flaming spiritual Sun into our hearts. Eventually through their work, all depression and hopelessness can be overcome with the sheer intensity of faith and power we derive from them.

A meditation on the second ray

White Eagle has said that those who respond to the second ray, that of philanthropy or altruism, are always working under the ray of love. He says: 'The people of the second ray are servers—ready at all times to serve because of the spirit of love dominant in them'. In the one who seeks to be attuned to the angels of the orange ray, then, the inner voice will resound with prayer similar in spirit to that of St Francis: 'Lord, make me an instrument of thy peace.... Grant that I may seek not so much to be consoled, as to console....'

In meditation, when you reach the centre of the garden, or the temple, or when you recognize the Master or divine Mother in the heart of the rose or the lotus flower and receive into your heart their blessing, what happens is that you only long to give and to serve. No other course is open to you, for in touching that heart of divine love you know, as did the Buddha, that you are one with all, and all life is interdependent. Your pain is mine; your joy is my joy. The angels are called by the longing in your heart to help others; and they bring an increased empathy and compassion to you. The intuition is strengthened and opened in order that you may understand and give wisely. During this time in communion with them in the heart of the rose or lotus, you experience the radiation of love, like the golden rays from a sun or the perfume of a flower, flowing outwards endlessly to all, bringing healing from all suffering.

A meditation on the third ray

Of people who respond to the third ray, of wisdom, White Eagle has said this: 'They like to be their own teachers; to experience life and make their own contacts, and not depend upon what another teacher tells them. They are philosophical, adaptable to circumstances, and when fully developed will not be overcome by circumstances, but master any condition in which they find themselves. They are true philosophers'. He has also said that this yellow ray is very beautiful.

Here we have an aspect of wisdom which is essential to all being, namely that we have to learn for ourselves. This means that we truly believe and know with our deepest soul, and can stand firm in the face of all criticism and opposition. This is the ray of truth and uniqueness, and if one seeks to be in harmony with the angels of this yellow ray, then the call in our hearts must be: 'Lord, make me fearless to follow the path of tolerance'. The deepest truth and learning always leads to a much greater understanding and tolerance, whereas limited judgments by the earthly mind are often made out of ignorance and fear.

Sometimes one is led to a temple of wisdom during meditation. The floor of this temple may be a pattern of black and white squares, symbolizing the balance of new learning and its consolidation, in other words light and darkness. The guardian angel, who holds the karma of the life, can pull aside the veil and reveal to one's eyes the record of the soul's growth through many lives (which White Eagle calls the Akashic record) kept by the recording angels. In the shelter and warmth of this temple, and in the supportive embrace of the guardian, one is made aware of far deeper guiding reasons and promptings behind the actions of people on earth. One sees through to the heart of things, to the reason for sufferings and sorrows; and the deepest humility comes to the soul. The angels of the yellow ray, those of the spiritual philosopher, can touch the soul with an understanding for others which is beyond words to describe. The soul's understanding then embraces the interconnectedness of all the divine laws. It knows how each soul lives out in its lives a unique aspect of divinity, and how each touches and enhances the whole.

A meditation on the fourth ray
The green ray of harmony lies at the heart of the star, at the centre of the rays.

POWER
LOVE
WISDOM
———— HARMONY ————
WISDOM
LOVE
POWER

The angels of this fourth ray help us to express higher things in form. In other words, they help us to create, and to bring forth into material life the aspects of the divine. It is interesting that this is the green ray—the colour of growth and rebirth, the colour of beginning again. When we seek to contact these angels at a time of beginning, we may find ourselves saying within: 'May I learn to lay aside the past;

to let go of all that is unnecessary and unworthy, and to open to new life, to a pure and balanced spiritual purpose'.

As we enter the garden in meditation, or behold the wonderful vision of nature in all its manifestations in the world of spirit, the feeling of life, vitality and infinite possibilities for creation and for good that comes to us is intoxicating. The very air one breathes in these places in the spirit is like wine, but pure and fresh and exhilarating. All the verdant growth radiates a light which sparkles with creative force, yet all is in harmony. Even where the garden is wonderfully wild there is an awareness of balance and integrity: nothing jars, or seems out of place.

In contact with the angels of the green ray, one is aware of becoming centred and still, even within the heart of movement and life and creation. There is an awareness of complete attunement and at-one-ment with the divine plan. All is flowing as it should; everything has its place and its time. With such a feeling there comes complete peace. One perhaps finds oneself simply sitting beneath a tall tree and watching the elementals playing in the sunlight, or lying on the warm grass listening to birdsong and the soft wind. A great feeling of contentment steals over the soul as the angels of harmony bring the awareness of the rightness of all life.

Once experienced in meditation, this feeling of contentment and peace profoundly influences the daily life. With equanimity comes intelligence and clear sight, the ability to see what is appropriate; the angels of harmony enable the mind of earth to feel the inspiration of the spirit and give it form. It is as if one retains the sweet air of the eternal garden, and can breathe it out upon the earth in creative response to all conditions, and into new life and new creations of beauty and imagination.

With the next three rays we find more of a blending of the great principles of wisdom, love and power. Eventually, they all meet as one in God. In responding to these rays we are reminding ourselves that there is no true wisdom without love, and that the two in turn bring great power into manifestation; or that love and wisdom need the will to bring them to life and to sustain them.

A meditation on the fifth ray

The fifth ray is the blue ray, which is a colour of devotion. White Eagle has referred to it as the ray of science, but also of devotional power. He says: 'Try to find a wide and universal conception of blue. Those who respond to this ray like to get to the very cause of things, and are devoted to truth'. The angels of the blue ray bring the qualities of power, peace and strength, and White Eagle adds: 'Those who worship or pray in truth will be seen to project rays of blue and these thought-forms will take very beautiful shape also. You will therefore understand why the blue is used so much in prayer groups'. In the absent healing service in his Lodge the following words, inspired by White Eagle himself, are used at the beginning of the ritual wording: 'With the aid of angels we shall put into operation a law of healing, precise, definite, certain and scientific'. The words describe very well an element of the work of the angels of the blue ray.

In meditation we may find ourselves with a group of brethren on the inner planes, sitting in a circle round a healing pool of clear, blue water. The feeling generated by this circle of brethren is one of purity of thought and emotion, clarity of mind, and deep commitment to the divine plan; so that the water of the pool is completely still and pure, perfectly reflecting the Christ Sun or Star. Around these brethren the angels stand, their auras forming the pillars of a temple. No words are spoken, yet great power for good is radiating into the world.

A meditation on the sixth ray

The sixth ray is the indigo ray of love and true mysticism. White Eagle has referred to the keynote of the sixth ray as 'true goodness'.

'People who respond to the sixth ray always know that God is good, God is omnipotent, so that this is the ray of religious aspiration.'

Just as indigo is a colour both subtle and profound, so in seeking to attune to the angels of the sixth ray one has to seek to let go of all pettiness, 'all isolation of self' (another phrase from the White Eagle absent healing service), and seek to be mindful in all things. Many people have made the mistake of thinking that to shut themselves away from the world entirely is the only way to achieve this deep mystical rapport and understanding. Yet from White Eagle's teaching we can see that responding with 'true goodness' to life is the way of the active mystic, as with all great masters. Their lives show this incontrovertible connection between simple goodness towards all, and the power of the mystic. White Eagle has referred to the Master Jesus as head of the indigo ray, and Jesus' life certainly demonstrated this.

In meditation, the angels of the indigo ray will appear in the deepest silence and stillness, when love for God and all good is the only thought in the mind, the only desire in the heart. Here the feeling of awe and reverence is intensified. It is almost as if the longing for God has produced a state of emptiness—empty of self, freed from the confines, restrictions and narrowness of the earthly thought—and the heart is set free to merge with the Creator at a much more profound level. One may find oneself gazing at the immensity of a sky full of stars, from a place high in the mountains, or into the deep blue waters of a still forest pool, surrounded by trees. One may feel the contact with these angels at any time when the sense of wonder and oneness is there. Sometimes one may for a short while be able to look into the eyes of the Beloved.

No words can truly describe this state of being, but once it is touched, the earthly life is transformed, for one is able to see the mystical quality of love behind all physical manifestations and in the hearts of all people. Nothing is ever quite so boring or ordinary again!

A meditation on the seventh ray

Though it is normally seen as the ray of ceremonies and ritual, White Eagle has called the seventh ray the ray of beauty, and of true spiritual power. This is the violet ray, and blends the blue of devotion with the red of will. Through the influence of the angels of this ray, one calls down the great spiritual power to baptize the earth. White Eagle says: 'The people on this ray, loving beauty, loving music, loving colour, draw to themselves angelic beings who give power for such ceremonies'.

The indescribable mystical contact we can make through the indigo ray, by the will of God and because of this love in the heart, enables us in a greater degree to bring the Christ-power to earth. This is divine magic. Sometimes in meditation we may find ourselves taking part in a great ceremony on the inner planes—perhaps in one of the ancient stone circles, which on the inner planes reveal the power of the light in the stones. The angels who assist in these ceremonies are majestic and radiant.

At any time in meditation when we respond to the beauty which is to be found on the inner planes, we touch the aura of the angels of the seventh ray. There are an infinite number of ways in which one may be moved by loveliness in this inner world. It may be something as simple as gazing into the heart of a flower, or of watching the elementals at play in the rolling waves of the sea. Beauty, and the response to it, opens the heart in a way which is beyond our knowledge. Yet power is intensified by beauty's expression, and the great devas respond to this aspect of God. One feels their harmonizing presence, and in daily life this contact enables more divine light to penetrate the mists of earth, and bring harmony to earthly conditions. Where there is beauty and harmony all is good, for all the rays are balanced. The Christ light becomes manifest.

14. Continual Genesis

White Eagle has given us a picture of the continual genesis of what he calls 'lifestreams' which flow from the heart of the spiritual Sun. They are streams of 'vital force' which exist behind physical life in the etheric and on the higher planes. This life-force in its different streams is responsible for the growing God-consciousness and evolution in all the myriad life of earth. 'Lifestream' is synonymous neither with the physical life nor with the angelic life, but rather, it is the etheric foundation *for* that life. When White Eagle talks later in this chapter about the different paths of development, these are not the same as the physical evolution of life-forms studied by our scientists. It may also help to be clear that there is a difference between 'lifestreams' and 'life in form', though the one animates and gives spiritual life to the other.

The passage of teaching chosen for this chapter is longer than that in most chapters of this book, and I feel that White Eagle has given so extended a picture of the immense and almost incomprehensible background to physical life, to help us recognize just how limited our conception of life can be. Our minds may then expand to the awareness of a more vast and magical universe—an eternal, ever-growing cosmic life. In the process we may become less rigid in our thinking and more tolerant of the different manifestations of

spiritual truth. White Eagle's account of the lifestreams also helps us
to see just how on this etheric level the angels, nature and human
evolution are all linked.

Can you picture lifestreams whirling forth from the central
Sun, and returning again: a continual movement, a continual vibration? The spiritual seeds of life—of which you
are one—come pouring forth into this cycle of life, vibrating, pulsating, evolving, and ever slowly but surely growing
in consciousness of their true nature, ever growing in God-
consciousness.

We would emphasize the stupendous life-force which
streams upon the earth plane. Behind every manifestation
in physical matter there exists, both on the etheric and on
the higher planes (astral, mental, and spiritual) a corresponding vibration of life. Conceive this magnificent outpouring
upon the earth plane as streams of life-force, streams of vital force, outpourings of the God-life. That is how life is
initiated. As the lifestream descends into the lowest strata of
form life, for instance into the mineral kingdom, a new round
of life is heralded, whether in the earth or in the bed of the
ocean. Once etheric life has followed this descending path
of evolution, it turns and climbs again, opening and branch-
ing, until there is ultimate expression or manifestation in the
adept (the perfect man or woman), or in the angel being.
Such an angel being has the task of directing and helping
the evolving forms of life along the path upon which he or
she has already travelled. Thus the higher levels of life can
be separated into two, the angelic and the human.

Shall we divide life into two main lines of development?
There is the sea 'and all that therein is', and the earth, com-
mencing with the mineral kingdom. You may marvel at the

rock formation of the earth, and be impressed by the beauty of precious stones found therein; yet behind all physical form is the etheric facsimile. In the etheric are forms of life, not fairies or nature spirits, but etheric formations which live in the very substance of the earth. These are the lowest forms of etheric life to which we can refer.

From that lowest mineral form of life we pass to the fungoid growth. This again has behind it its own etheric form; and we pass to the insect, and onwards to the reptile and bird life. When the life-form reaches a certain stage it merges into the form life which results from some other lifestream. For instance, having reached the bird stage, the life essence takes form as the fairy, or the nature spirit. Life at this stage sheds the material life-form, and takes an astral formation, as well as an etheric. Such forms of life manifest in etheric and astral matter, not physical. The astral body is one of feeling, emotion, so that at this stage we find affection; these nature spirits feel affection and respond to love—or the reverse.

The other path is the watery one. Shall I trace it for you? We commence with the forms of life in the bed of the ocean. In the ocean itself there are such etheric forms, not seen but living in the water. You might group them together and call them water spirits, or water sprites. A life-form dwells in the coral, a form of life which little etheric creatures work through, and inhabit. The next stage upwards is into the fish and the higher forms of life in the sea. The higher aspects of this water life manifest in the etheric forms of the clouds. Witness the extraordinary formation of the clouds. It is caused by the wind, you may say: and yet not wholly—all such manifestations have behind them the busy work and the games of the creatures of the air.

Let us consider another lifestream (we are giving you just

a few out of the many). Consider the grass; the myriad little lives of grass. From the grass the next step is the corn, from which comes the bread of life; a step further, and we reach the ant-life, and the life of the bees. From the vegetable kingdom of the flowers, the shrubs and the trees, the lifestream passes into the mammals, the animal form. It goes from the lower types into the domestic animal; from the domestic animal into the lowest human stratum, and onwards to the adept.

Do not mistake me, a beautiful and beloved tree does not come back as, say, a disagreeable animal; this is not quite the idea. Think of the strata of life in terms of *lifestreams* ever pouring down, ever shaping into certain grades or life-forms. The lifestream which has produced a beloved and beautiful tree can in the next manifestation take form as a loved animal—a dog perhaps.

At a certain stage, when that beloved dog dies, through the love and contact with its human companions during its life, it should have absorbed that which raises it to the point at which it receives what I will describe as the divine spark. This is the outpouring of the wisdom aspect of the deity, and gives to the entity the consciousness of God; the knowledge of good and evil.

At that stage the dog passes from one lifestream to the next, and is able to receive sufficient of divine intelligence to give it a measure of freewill. Whereas before it acted purely by direction of the master mind of the lifestream—the nature spirit in control of that stream—when it passes to the human, it is free to choose whether it will respond to the God- or the self-will. (We must remember, however, that evolution first requires the self-will in order to develop the ego or the individual.) When this power of decision or choice is given to the individualized spirit, karma starts.

Behind all these physical forms are corresponding etheric forms, until we get to the stage where the astral form
comes into being. You find this, as we have said before, at
the level of the bird life. Here you get the nature spirits—
the fairies—and from the fairies the next life-form (all fairies in reality): the salamanders or fire spirits, and then the
air spirits. From the air spirits comes evolution to the lower
angelic plane. The lower angels have many air sylphs in their
service, and help them in their evolution, even as humanity
helps the domestic animals onwards in their evolution.
Through their work and service to the scheme of evolution
these lesser angels receive this outpouring of wisdom and
become blessed with separate consciousness. They, too, cease
to be controlled by the group mind and become individualized and advance into the angel kingdom.

Rarely, but occasionally, we get a crossing over from the
nature line of evolution into the human. It has been known
for angels to take human form. It is not usual, but if it is
necessary for any particular purpose, then it is done. Also, a
person who has arrived at that point where he or she becomes an adept, a perfect man or woman, has a choice. He
or she may follow the angelic line of growth and service,
and become one of the solar angels. There are, in the higher
strata of the invisible, great solar beings who visit such a
planet as the earth (and others too), at times when they need
help, and bring their light and their power to help on and
upward the great earth stream of life.

How long does all this take? Do not think that all the life
evolving in the mineral, in the sea, in the vegetable, is for
manifestation on this earth. Rather, you should consider that
life is being prepared for a planet too far distant in time for

us even to contemplate, even as the life today results from a globe of countless millions of years ago. For at the apex of life there comes a blending, or cooperation, a completion of the scheme of creation, in the solar universe. We can even go further, and visualize that beyond this life-round, the beings of perfected life pass onwards through other planets, until they bear their part in the completion of yet another system of worlds, another solar system. Genesis tells you of seven great days: but not of twenty-four hours, rather periods of countless years, each 'day' serving to create or bring into form one of the seven lifestreams.

The whole process is so slow and so grand it is impossible at this stage to get a comprehensive view of it All you can do is appreciate that behind all physical form is this wonderful and beautiful invisible etheric life. When you thus open your vision to see the little people at work, and view the glorious panorama of God's love, God's beauty manifest everywhere, you will help the whole scheme by intelligent recognition of, and intelligent cooperation with, the fairies and nature spirits.

There are many lifestreams under the control of the angel kingdom; countless small people, small spirits who look to the human family for human love. It is the human or Christ love which only the humans have been given as a special gift from their Father–Mother God that can help the little people in the nature kingdoms. Even angels themselves draw help from the Christ love manifesting through the human character and life.

Yet all these different aspects of life belong to the one Great Spirit, and for the progress and evolution of the human spirit, it is necessary to include these other kingdoms, for all move forward together as a great chain of life—all kingdoms are links in the chain, and all are attached to the supreme trinity of life: wisdom, love and power.

When we read the above passages about the lifestreams, intellectually, we may be struck with a sense of complexity and find the subject difficult to understand. However (as I mentioned earlier in the book), there is a level of awareness at which we can, for a moment, *feel* the sense of connection and of oneness White Eagle describes. Then it is as if our consciousness has expanded to the extent that we are no longer identifying with the body we inhabit, but feel part of the spiritual lifestream in nature. This can happen during meditation, but also, sometimes, when experiencing nature: when we are swimming in a warm blue sea, climbing a mountain, walking in dappled sunlight under blossoming trees, catching a glimpse of dolphins or seals, or watching the deer in the heart of the forest. This is the level at which we connect with the angelic realm: because we slip into this immense stream of consciousness which is beneath everyday life.

15. Vibrating in Harmony with the Planets

Sceptics may question how a lump of rock millions of miles away can affect the human personality. Nonetheless White Eagle's account of the planetary angels enables us to witness the hidden astrological energies. He reminds us that part of the work of the planetary angels is to help bring through energies from the seven great rays to influence the etheric lifestreams in the development of God-consciousness.

The minerals and precious stones are a mass of vibration, and all flowers and vegetables are too. If you could see with clear vision across the moorlands, or even in your garden, you would see a mass of magnificent colour and life, pulsating, vibrating; you would see the little fairy people working to weave the harmony of life in nature, producing the beautiful colour and perfume of the flowers. Although you cannot smell the perfume in some flowers, nevertheless that perfume exists, but you may not be attuned to its particular vibration. And so with music. If you could enter the spirit life you would be arrested by the perfume and the music which fills the atmosphere. The colours of the flowers each have their own sound: they play the harmony of God.

Moreover, not only are all these kingdoms vibrating with

colour, music and perfume, but interpenetrating all the earth life are the rays of the planets; as, too, there are parts of your body which can vibrate in harmony with certain planets. As we tread the path of evolution, so we strive to understand and receive more fully into our being these vibrations of life. When a soul has learnt to vibrate harmoniously with all forms of life, then it has attained mastership.

We ask those of you who have not yet become conscious of the power of the planetary influences over the earth, to endeavour to realize their presence, their influence, and the blessings which these angelic forces are pouring forth upon humanity. The angel messengers from other planets come to strengthen your higher bodies. They work with you, enabling you to send forth, to other human beings, strong and clear rays of light. No light is wasted, because it is reflected and it will return to you and cause your higher and subtler bodies to become pure and strong and receptive and active upon the higher planes of your life.

The messengers, or angelic ones, from Mercury are becoming very active at the present time. The influence that comes from them is to help you attain self-mastery. In your daily life, if you will respond to these angelic ones, that self-mastery will direct you to attain perfection in action, in thought, in attunement to the cosmos.

The messengers who come to help humanity from the planet Venus bring harmony into your life, harmony into the centre of your being. These angels embrace and bring wisdom, for the angels of Venus are so lovely, they are all-love and beauty. Self-mastery, harmony and love—the wisdom and the love of the angels of Mercury and Venus—have the greatest power for the perfecting of the human race.

Then there are those silent recorders, the angels of Saturn, whom we would call the angels of the light. They will not let a soul pass onwards until it has learnt the exact and precise lesson which must be learnt. Angels of Saturn move slowly and surely, but they help humanity reap a goodly harvest, rich and golden. The angels from Saturn and Mercury are so brilliant.

The angels of Uranus sound the trumpet call; they come sweeping through, bringing a breaking-up of solid conditions which have been crystallized and set by Saturn. This cleansing and purification is an aspect of God perhaps not yet understood by the young in spirit. If things are swept out of your life, know that all is constructive, all is good. Work in harmony with the forces of God, and see in everything construction, evolution, growth and beauty.

Then the work of the angels of Mars is of the utmost value to human kind, bringing stimulation, bringing increased light, bringing the courage and the energy which you all need to progress on the path. The angels of Jupiter, who are now coming into closer contact with the earth, stand with the scales and bring law and order, and through their influence a wonderful beneficent power is absorbed by those souls who are particularly attuned to the vibrations of Jupiter.

As we have already explained, it is impossible to deal adequately with these profound truths. We ourselves have only caught a glimpse of the grandeur of the universe: only a glimpse of the possibilities which lie within us all. But each time you endeavour to reach the high places of the heavenly light, you are making a contact with powerful angelic forces, for in each one of you is the magnetic attraction by which you are brought into tune with angelic power, with a planetary ray. These rays are experienced in different degrees, but in you, individually, lies the power to attract and absorb into your being your own particular planetary forces.

You will find help in attuning to these planetary angels in Joan Hodgson's book PLANETARY HARMONIES, in which she gives morning and evening meditations for each day of the week. They are partly based upon the Essene communions, but also arise out of her own astrological experience and meditation. Each meditation is linked to the angel whose vibration is felt that day at sunrise and sunset.

Joan also describes the work of the planetary angels at the time of birth. 'The planetary angels, through the signs of the zodiac, act under the laws of karma to bring to the incarnating soul exactly the conditions of mind, body and environment which have been earned and which will give the best opportunity for future development.

'As soon as conception takes place the planetary beings within the soul's own universe begin to build the various bodies. The creation of the body for the incoming soul, the division of the cells and their organization under the influence of these planetary builders, is a miracle—a mystery at present beyond human understanding.

'Since the planetary beings in charge of the growing embryo are part of the universe of the incoming soul, the karmic conditions of that soul are being interwoven in the physical cells as they develop within the womb of the mother, to whom the soul has been drawn through past experiences. The child is born at the exact moment when the planetary conditions in the outer world are precisely aligned to those of the world within. Thus the horoscope at birth is a mirror of the soul with its past, present and future potentialities.'*

*ASTROLOGY THE SACRED SCIENCE *(White Eagle Publishing Trust, 1978), p. 20. For further details of Joan Hodgson's astrological work, write to the publisher.*

16. Guarded and Guided by Angels

Perhaps the overwhelming tenderness and awe which we may feel when we are present at the birth of a child (and also at someone's death) is because the angels are near. They draw particularly close at these times; just as the baby comes into incarnation accompanied by his or her guardian angel. White Eagle says:

> We would have you conceive of the spiritual realms as spheres of life, of form, of beauty reaching from earth to the highest heights of heaven. Yet even the highest heights can be contacted from the earth. Spiritual beings can descend through the planes or make a link through some harmonious channel until they contact a man or woman on the physical plane. The humblest child of God is not without his or her guardian angel. The chakras of your etheric body are focal points through which these guides and angelic helpers make their contact.
>
> At the time of a person's birth, and even before the actual birth of the baby, the guardian angel is at work. It is actually when the soul takes the decision to reincarnate that it comes under the care of the guardian angel. As it draws nearer to its future parents the way is prepared spiritually.

The guardian angel is concerned with the formation of the physical body. But there at the human birth is not only the angel but also the presence in form of divine Mother. The guardian angel remains with the soul during the whole of its life, and when the soul passes onward receives the soul in the spirit world.

The guardian angel works under the direction of the lords of karma, because the soul in its charge has come back in order to pay its karmic debts and thereby to learn certain lessons. The guardian angel is there to inspire, guide and help, but never to force the soul. Humanity's gift of freewill is always respected. The soul must choose, but at the same time you get this helpful angelic influence.

So every soul has its own guardian angel (who is called the angel of records, because he or she is in touch with the lords of karma) as well as the companionship of its guide. As you come into your physical incarnation you are accompanied by the two of them, the angel and the guide. Cultivate the habit of trusting these two who are always with you. Walk your path in full consciousness of them, and give them your confidence, for they are God's messengers.

There is another part which the guardian angel has to play, which is linked with a person's karma. White Eagle describes it thus:

In the degree the soul responds to heavenly influences and is thereby advanced on the path, it will also be beset with human problems. You can respond to these difficulties—often in human relationships—either guided by the higher spiritual impulse, or by the instincts of the lower self. The guardian angel is the helper of the soul *when it desires to be helped*, and does so by guiding it, by strengthening it. Angels are God's messengers sent to help a person through spiritual experiences. Every time you respond to a higher, to a good, to a spiritual impulse, you are helped by your guardian angel.

A personal story may be helpful. I was trying to deal with a difficult situation, but my own negative feelings were getting in the way. I therefore kept asking for help to let go of these feelings, first of all in a vague way, and then by consciously asking White Eagle and my guide. However, what became clear to me after a while was that it is the guardian angel which helps us in such circumstances. I felt my guardian angel draw close—all stillness and equanimity and pure love—and as he did so, I was able to let go of the unhelpful feelings and get in touch with love again.

I will describe how this felt for me. Through my practice of White Eagle's method of meditation, I was aware of the angel's presence in a specific way (though at other times it could have been much more general). The sensation in my physical body was centred at the base of the head, near my throat chakra. I suppose this is because from a karmic point of view the throat chakra is the one which responds to the etheric on the level the angel can reach. A feeling of peace spread outwards from this centre, and with it, the colour of the angel— deep indigo blue in the main—seemed to encircle me.

What came to me was that the guardian angel brings to us, and helps us to meet, our karma and opportunities in life; and so, also, the angel has the wherewithal to help us transcend this karma when we truly wish to and are truly prepared to accept and let go.

When we struggle with any negative feelings—resentment, pain, tiredness, mental busy-ness, anything which is inhibiting the flow of love, the contact with love—and we truly wish to let go of these, but are finding it difficult, then our guardian angel will help us. Perhaps our true aspiration allows the angel the space and the permission (remembering our freewill) to flood our aura with their colour, which can reconnect us with our true, loving, peaceful self and our true soul purpose. In SPIRITUAL UNFOLDMENT I, White Eagle has this to say about the guardian angel:

> Your guardian angel never leaves you. From the moment of your entering upon mortal life to the time when you leave it, and even afterwards, your guardian angel is in touch with you. It is concerned with your karma and directs your life under the control of the lords of karma. The angel is impersonal in the sense that its work is to see that you are guided towards opportunities to pay off karmic debts, or opportunities to earn good karma to add to the credit of your account. Thus every experience is an opportunity.... But when you *do* fall down and everything is chaotic, remember that there is a helper by your side. Your guardian angel has seen your fall, but will not condemn. He or she does not say, 'I told you so!' Instead, there is a whisper within your heart, 'Courage.... I will help you rise again. Look up, look out! God is still in His heaven and all is well'.

On another occasion, White Eagle gave an interesting description of how the guardian angel can teach a soul on the inner planes:

> In the astral world a soul will sometimes meet its guardian angel in disguise, and, say, shrouded in darkness. The point is this: that every soul must attain complete confidence in God, knowing that whatever or whoever confronts it, God is present, therefore no harm can touch it. If the soul is firmly rooted in confidence in God, behind that disguise would be revealed a beautiful angel of light. So we all, deep within our souls, must know that behind every dark happening,

behind every difficulty, there is a hidden blessing. You all have to develop that faith, that confidence in God, and in divine magic, so that at the right moment—at the acceptable time of the Lord—the magic will be worked, the dark shroud will fall away, and behind will be the radiant angel—the glory of God's life.

Finally, I should like to describe an event from the life of a member of the White Eagle Lodge in Switzerland. What follows is a very moving story which he shared with us, and which seems to reflect what has been said about guardian angels.

It concerns an accident which happened to him as a young man and affected all the rest of his life. He was a technician working in a chemical laboratory in London at the time and one day he went into the laboratory alone to inspect some work there. As he went through the door he saw unmistakably an angel form, and as he looked he saw that the angel, with a feeling of great tenderness and compassion, was covering its face with its hands. A few minutes later, as he examined the apparatus, the chemicals exploded in his face, permanently blinding him. This is not the place to tell the story of the rest of his life, but he went on, with his wife's help, to do most beautiful spiritual work which, it is no exaggeration to say, touched the lives of thousands, and which it is most unlikely he would have done had he had his sight. The understanding we have of this story is that the angel did not warn him in a way which would definitely have prevented the accident, since maybe this traumatic incident was part of his life's purpose. However, the angel, which we must feel was his guardian angel, made itself known with total awareness and tenderness; to show him that whatever happened it was there and would carry his soul through this turning point in his life.

17. Angels Hold the Balance

The story given at the end of the last chapter gives much reassurance of the love in which we are all held, and the exactness and rightness of the plan for each human life. Most important was the man's reaction to his blindness—it deepened and strengthened both his own spiritual contact, and his desire to serve and help others. What could have been seen as only a darkness and a disaster, became, through his response to it and that of his wife also, a beacon of light for others.

This leads us to the subject of this chapter. The words from White Eagle given on pages 119–20 were taken from a talk on the subject of good and evil, which is, as he says, 'the law of karma'. The book SPIRITUAL UNFOLDMENT II has a whole chapter devoted to White Eagle's teaching on the subject of the angels of darkness and the angels of light. We are reminded of the importance of this subject when we consider how closely the angels—particularly those who are guardians and healing angels—work under the guidance of the lords of karma, bringing to the soul those conditions which will enable the greatest learning and the greatest opportunities for service (sometimes, as in the quotation which follows, in the guise of evil).

Many people fear evil, therefore they want to attack it. But evil, as we have told you before, is only overcome by good. Evil is a form of undeveloped, undisciplined good. The two great opposites, so-called good and evil, are like great wheels working one within another to bring about spiritual evolution, to bring forth ultimate beauty and perfection from life. What the world calls evil is, in reality, a great force which is training humanity to recognize the divine truth that God is love. So-called evil provides a pressure, or becomes a test to a person's soul, to keep him or her on the path.

Evil is likened to the angel with a sword placed at the gate of the garden of Eden, paradise, or nirvana. The angel draws a ring with her sword of light, and only those who have been tried and tested and are become as pure gold, can pass onward. The great angels of darkness, like Lucifer (which means light), eventually bring out all that is finest in a soul's nature.

White Eagle elsewhere gives us very important advice about how to deal with this opposing, yet necessary, force. He says:

Many people concern themselves too much with what they call evil and darkness, until such thoughts become an obsession. Such people are continually combating forces of evil and darkness. It is, however, necessary to view the two aspects of good and evil dispassionately: to see them as opposing forces which, by their opposition, help to maintain the world on its course. We may liken the two to centripetal and centrifugal force, since the one is the driving out and the other is the turning in, or driving in. The evil appears to be the one which is driving in, and so we liken this force to selfishness. Great human selfishness tends to draw everything to itself, while unselfishness, or love, is projecting, is radiating light, and is the recreating element. You have perfect freewill to approach this great problem as you are urged. We ourselves, however, would rather concentrate upon the angels of light, goodness and love, instead of upon evil.

In passing, however, let us add that evil is very difficult to define. Often it is a question of geography: what might be considered bad in a Christian country can be practised elsewhere with impunity. So-called 'primitive' peoples may have a different code of conduct. What they believe right might appear to others to be really bad. Moreover, many social practices which have been accepted quite happily for centuries in your country now appear to the enlightened and awakened soul of this age as being very wrong. So it is necessary to take a wise and very broad view of the whole.

Also, every human being is an individual; everyone passes through his or her own individual experiences; every soul reacts to those experiences in its own particular way. You are not all cast in one mould. That is why no-one can judge another soul. It is also impossible for us to judge. *We do not judge.* Indeed, we dare not judge any living soul. We know certain spiritual laws exist; and we know what disobedience or obedience to these cosmic laws will entail, but we do not, we *cannot* criticize another person for taking their own unique path to heaven.

18. Birth and Death: the Angels of Divine Mother

Although I have created this separate chapter in which to share a little of White Eagle's teaching about divine Mother, it has to be remembered that her influence is felt through all life and all aspects of the angelic work. As White Eagle has said, the angels are connected with all creation of form; they create using the soul attributes, and because they create they all work within the aura of divine Mother—the ultimate creator of the form of all life.

White Eagle gives us a most powerful description of the essence of the work of this great being, who we think of as the second ray of the trinity. He says:

When we refer to the presence in form of the great Mother spirit some of you may wonder what we mean. This perfect human form, with feet on the ground, body erect, vision into the heavens and arms outstretched in the form of a cross to serve all life, is a most powerful figure. For when a being stands like this, when the cross is made, considerable power radiates into the ether, into the soul of the world. The ether is drawn up and moulded by the power of good thought or God-thought from the great Mother of life—the divine Mother. This great spirit who is part of the heavenly

Father is a great spiritual force, and She draws to Herself substance so that, by the power of Her thought and the creative angels, form is built in the soul world. That form remains in these higher ethers, so long as it is accomplishing what it is meant to do.

We are particularly aware of divine Mother's presence and power when we contemplate the natural world and all the generation and regeneration of life, colour, perfume and harmony which she and her angels bring into being.

At both the beginning and end of all creation divine Mother and the angels are present. This is particularly true, of course, at the birth of a baby. White Eagle says, 'Not a child is born which is unattended by the company of the divine Mother and her angelic band at the time of birth'. But they are also present when someone passes into the world of light (which is also a birth—a rebirth—into the world of spirit). White Eagle refers to the angels present at these times as the angels of life and death, and all come under the ultimate guidance of the feminine aspect of the deity, divine Mother. You will find more of his teaching about this in SPIRITUAL UNFOLDMENT II, but in the following rather lovely passage you can hear him saying directly to the students before him what magic these angels weave, and how the angel of death is not the 'gruesome spectre' we sometimes imagine:

Some of you can tranquilly say that all fear of death has now passed, and you can truly look through the very thin veil into that larger, spiritual life, with complete confidence and indeed with joyful anticipation. You can also rejoice instead of grieve when one of your number has been visited by the angels of the great Mother. You can picture the great Mother as coming at the appointed time and her angels drawing the bolt which bars the door between this world and the next. We would have you remember also the joy with which your loved one goes forth into a garden of sunlight and perfumed flowers as the door is flung wide.

Whenever a soul is leaving its body the angel of death is there with that soul, and lesser angels carry the soul tenderly upwards into the spheres of light. The shell left behind is not your loved one, who has risen on angels' wings into a world of beauty.

I asked my husband Jeremy to contribute to this book a description of a dying process he had witnessed, namely the passing of Minesta—Grace Cooke, White Eagle's medium. He writes:

'The first death of someone really close to me was that of my grandmother when I was in my twenties. I had been involved very much in looking after her in the previous months and was there for much of the time in the last three days before her passing. She had been looked after in her own bedroom at home and we had all become very familiar with the little routines of nursing and general care. As those who have been through this process will know, this all builds up a slightly busy, almost hospital-like atmosphere.

'The strange thing was that a couple of days before her passing we knew that a process was under way, even though there was no outward change, because somehow the atmosphere and energy in the room had changed. Instead of the outward brightness, we gradually became aware of a growing stillness in her room. It was almost like an energy underneath the daily activity which was still going on. When we went into her room we felt that something not sad, but very earnest and composed, was happening.

'It was really as if the angels were there, quietly and without emotion, making the pathway for her soul's transition. In the final hours of her life it seemed to me as if all her being was drawn into a ball of light right in her heart, just as though it was a childlike readiness for departure; and all the time the presence was there, so tender, so still— in its own way so powerful.

'After the moment of her actual passing her face looked in one way just the same, but in a very tangible way it was just the empty form. My own reaction at the time was not of grief; I felt totally hushed, and in the deepest way privileged to have been part of what felt like a holy and sacred process, and yet one which was also so natural and human. The emotions around her passing came later but, looking back now, the strongest memory of her passing, and the thing to which I can still go back in feeling, is of being touched by this beautiful, still, earnest work of the angels, in carrying a soul from the physical life into the world of light.'

19. Earth, Air, Fire and Water

White Eagle often refers to the angels of the elements when talking to healers within the White Eagle Lodge, or indeed to anyone who would be involved in healing (transforming darkness into light) wherever the need: individuals, humanity, our animal brethren, or the very earth herself. He says:

> Each human being has within them the four elements: earth, water, air and fire, and has separate bodies or vehicles through which he or she can contact the worlds of those elements. For example, the world of fire is directly connected with the solar force, the Sun-power, and also with the heart and with the spirit of a human being ... the son–daughter of God, the I AM; the sunlight, the love within the human soul. This power is the same power which can create universes. In a human being it can transform a life from darkness to light.
>
> It will help you in your work if you will think of the angels of the four elements, earth, air, fire and water. They will immediately come to your assistance when you call upon them, if you have attuned yourselves to them by purifying your thoughts and your physical body. Think, for instance,

of the angels of the water element. Picture the little people in the water: see them in the rain, and in the water as it moves and bubbles over the stones of the river; watch them in the movement of the sea; watch the movement and the life in the water, and remember, water is the life-giver and the cleanser. Think of the cleansing process of the water, the life-giving power it has, and of the angelic forces which use that power to cleanse and purify.

Welcome the angels of the air. When you take a walk in the country, breathe in the air and think of the angels of the air element, and the spirits of the air. Remember that they are all about you; they are the very life in the air and they will help you and revivify you. Breathe deeply, thinking of those angels of the air and the air spirits who are with you to purify and heal you—to bring you life and refreshment.

Think of the angels of fire, the angels of the sun. If you have developed your inner vision or your power of clear sight, you will see in the dancing sunlight these angels of fire: friendly, warming, healing. But always remember that the angels of fire expect love in your heart. Love is the vehicle, shall we say, of these angels of the fire element.

And, finally, think of the angels of the earth, and of the little elementals of the flowers, of the earth, the servers of the great mother nature. In your meditations, when you close your eyes and use your power of imagery, you can see these delightful nature spirits working under the direction of the great angels, and the power of the great mother of the earth. All those who love mother earth—horticulturists, agriculturalists, animal lovers, those who love the soil—all draw to themselves many nature spirits of the earth and the air.

When you work to alleviate pain and abolish cruelty; when you work amongst men and women to impress them with the beautiful light of the Christ-spirit; even when you create and cultivate a beautiful bed of flowers, or a lawn; or when you help to gather together and purify the water of the earth, you are contacting the angels of the elements. You live and work surrounded by all these wonderful beings. Listen to the song of the angels, the joy and happiness of the angels. Smell the perfume of the angels of mother earth, the perfume of the air, the water, the sun and the grass. Train yourself to become aware of and friendly with the nature spirits, friendly with the angels of the four elements; because if you work with them it will increase your power to heal.

In approaching the invisible worlds a person has to hold a pure love in his or her heart, first of all for human kind, and then for all creation. You have to love the elementals, for they play a very big part in helping the Master in his work for humanity. As you advance there must come peace, friendship and harmony between human beings and the elementals. You have a demonstration of this vital truth in the miracles of the Master Jesus. We are particularly thinking of the miracles of Jesus walking upon the water and stilling the storm. The walking on the water symbolized his complete control of the water element, the emotions—for the water elementals affect the emotions. He did not sink. His brothers, the water spirits, supported him, and he in turn was able to support his disciple while he held fast to trust and faith in his Master. The same thing happened when he stilled the storm. The air spirits, the sylphs, came to his assistance, and obeyed his command.

In order to obtain true mastery over the elements of earth, air, fire and water, you must become like the Son of God, all love, all tenderness, and therefore filled with the solar power.

You must win the respect and love of the beings of the elements. You are then making contact in your higher mind with the creative forces, for when you can value the services of brother air, brother water, brother sun and mother earth, when you can feel that you are part of the cosmic life, then you are becoming attuned to the divine life. You are like a sensitively attuned instrument. If you are pure in thought and speech and action, and if you strive to be simply good and simply kind, thanking God for your life and all its blessings, and for all the beauties of life—the beauties of the sunrise and of the sunsets, the beauties of the clouds and the skies—then you are becoming at one with the angels. So too, when you can enjoy the gentle rain without resentment for being wet, turning your face to these raindrops and thanking God, because this is life, and in all these elements are the angels, then you understand; and you are working hand in hand with the angels.

20. Healing: the Balancing of the Elements

In order to introduce the subject of healing, and how the angels of healing work through the chakras, White Eagle again refers to our relationship with the planets. He goes on to link the process of healing with that of building and creating form, something which takes us back to the subject-matter of the very first chapter.

A person is influenced all the time by the planets. These planetary influences play upon the human life through the chakras, which are the windows of the soul. Each chakra has a link with a planet and the colour associated with that planet; in turn governed by the Elohim, each at the head of their own particular ray.

Thus in healing a group is guided to use, mentally, certain rays of colour to heal. The rays bring harmony into the human body through the chakras: they restore what is lacking. Of course all people need healing in one form or another, for no-one is perfect yet. The disease, the dis-ease as we like to call it, shows in the physical body, of course; but it is the general vibrations, the harmony of the individual, which are disturbed. When an orchestra is out of tune, it gives pain. An orchestra must be most perfectly and exactly attuned, and the conductor must be *en rapport* with the orchestra if he or she would bring forth lovely harmonies.

Music is healing, because every ray, every colour of the spectrum, every planet, has its own particular tone, its own note upon which it vibrates; it, too, is being used by the angels to heal and to create.

Angelic ones present during healing ceremonies are not concerned only with healing some particular disease. That may sound rather unkind, but understand that they have perfect love and compassion for their lesser brethren. Behind any individual ministration by the healing angels there is always the grand plan of building. When the body is healed, when the angels help to purify and perfect the physical body, they do more than this; they create, they weave into the subtle vehicles and into the actual physical form, forces of light and spiritual power, destined slowly but surely to create and make ready the human form for the next race.

White Eagle was speaking to trained healers working in the White Eagle Lodge when he said:

We want to help you understand that you are channels for this cosmic power, this angelic power, this Christ-power. In healing you do not work alone; when you come into your healing groups, or when you are with a patient, remember the angels of healing—they are so real and they are close to you. It is by your love and your desire to give service that you are giving all that you possibly can to these messengers. You may not see the patient, but through your human agency the rays are linked by the angel bands, and the patient is able to receive that perfect and true healing power.

There are angels of all the colours which are sent forth:

angels of the violet ray, angels of the blue, and angels of the sun, the golden ray; angels of the green ray—the green of mother earth; angels of the sunlight, angels of joy, wisdom, love and power. According to the colour called by the leader, the angels of that particular colour gather round, and carrying the forces in them, they just go forth with your thought. Wherever that ray is directed, the angels work to carry the vibration to whatever part of the patient needs healing.

You are very often working blindfold, and therefore there is a great need for love, and faith—an inward knowing that you are working with these angelic powers; and although the angels may appear to be very impersonal, they are very strong in the particular quality or ray upon which they are working, upon which they are serving: the ray which is a contribution to the whole cosmic power.

The way you can develop your awareness and your fitness to be a clear and true channel for those angelic forces is by communing with God each day, if only for a short time. Just send your thanks to your Creator, and in the consciousness behind your human, active brain, just dwell in the knowledge that the angels are with you.

This simple, daily communion can take you right up through all the planes, water, air, fire, into the heavenly light, into that celestial world of the perfected sons and daughters of God. This is the path which the Aquarian Age opens up: beauty and harmony and brotherhood from earth to heaven. Then Jacob's ladder will be raised upon the earth, and every seeker who raises his or her body and opens their vision will see the angels coming and going between earth and heaven.

21. Ritual, Ceremonial and Sacred Places

This book has already touched on the importance of ritual, and the angels associated with the seventh ray of ceremonial. In the following passages White Eagle gives us descriptions of these angels—and the sacred sites at which important ceremonies take place—in such a way that he brings to life the grandeur of such occasions, yet he shows us how much the same sacredness is stimulated on earth by the simple love and devotion in our hearts.

All of you must learn to appreciate the importance of ceremonial and ritual. We do not mean merely undergoing a ceremony. We mean a comprehension of the invisible activity behind the ceremonies, which is used to stimulate your higher bodies so that you come into realization of the wonder of your true being.

So these feasts of remembrance were part of the ritual and part of the service of religions in the ancient days. These same forms and ceremonies will come back in a more powerful and more purified way and on even a higher vibration than before, because the earth is moving upward on the spiral of evolution, and so will receive more powerfully the blessing and help of the angelic ones and the Brotherhood of the Star.

When you come into a service in the White Eagle Lodge, the first thing for you to do is to close the doors of your soul to the outer world. As the ritual of your service proceeds, you are raised in consciousness from the physical level to an illumined and spiritual state of being. This is not only because of the words that we speak to you, but also you are helped by the preparation which has been going on from the moment the service started, or even before it started. In this preparation even the flowers play their part; the ritual of the music and the singing also helps invoke the angelic powers to build a spiritual temple around you. If you were clairvoyant you would see the angelic forms gathering; you would see three great beings clothed in white, yet reflecting all the soft colours of the spectrum, and you would see that these beings were acting as channels, directing golden and silver rays of light upon the congregation, raising it far above the worldly level of thought and feeling.

Thus ritual performed simply and with understanding not only helps to raise the consciousness of those participating, but also helps to create harmony, a channel through which the angels can send spiritual light to the earth people. You may go to a service with a mind full of material thoughts, or suffering, and by the ritual of the service and the help of the angels of ceremony, you are enabled to detach yourself from worldly things. With or without your conscious effort you are raised, and even if you cannot see them, you can feel the presence of angels, and go from the service uplifted and happy.

Ritual does not only take place in a church or in some gathering of people, but also within the individual being. As a service creates a channel for the inflow of the light of heaven, so also the ritual of the individual life can be a preparation for the reception and direction of the Great White

Light into the world. You can make the ritual of your life so perfect, so harmonious, that you are making yourself a channel for the light of the Christ-spirit, and are drawing to your aura angelic beings who will serve humanity through you. They will also serve *you*. This is why it is good and wise to live calmly and tranquilly. Haste and passion are destructive, and break down the fine vibrations of the soul temple which, by the quiet ritual of your life, you are endeavouring to build. Live calmly and you will be bringing into action a spiritual power which is creative.

If you have created such a channel within your being, you cannot live without your becoming a great server of humanity. Your name may not be shouted from the hilltops; you may pass from your body unknown and unsung. That does not matter, but what does matter is what you are giving to humanity, what you are creating in God's universe. If all men and women understood this truth and put it into practice, what a beautiful world you would have! 'Will perfection ever come?' you say. Our answer is, most certainly, for it is in the divine plan that you should learn to be a channel for the Great Spirit, should learn to create harmony, beauty and perfection. You are part of that universal spirit, and it is your work to manifest that light on earth.

White Eagle went on to say how much we have to thank the great souls of all time for the service they have rendered to humanity. Through their wise and loving use of ritual in their daily lives and in their ceremonies they have 'caused a great light to flood the earth. Were it not for such sainted lives the earth would not only be in a state of darkness, but would be destroyed'. When we visit ancient, sacred places, although the ceremonies on the outward level may be long gone, White Eagle reminds us that we can still sense, if we are patient and open, the impression these wonderful rituals have left upon the ether, and be aware of how they are still being performed in spirit.*

> When a group of sincere and holy brothers and sisters meet to practise the mysteries, as at the centres of power in your mystic isle of Britain, there is poured upon them a blazing golden light and, through them, into the very earth itself. The elementals of the earth, the nature and air spirits, as well as the angels themselves, for ages afterwards watch over that holy place, so that even the most insensitive folk are drawn thither. They do not know why. They think it is out of historical interest or because the centre is one of natural beauty. But we say there is within individuals a yearning, a spiritually magnetized point, which is attracted and drawn to such places. The mystic isle of Britain is called the mystic isle because it is full of these centres of pure spiritual power.
>
> There are temples, centres of power, and ancient stones all over the world: in Brittany, elsewhere in Europe, India, Egypt, ancient America, the Andes and in the Gobi desert. When a person of vision visits such a Sun temple his or her eyes are opened to see the great angels come close, drawn back to the scene of former ceremonies. Whenever a great ceremony has been performed anywhere, be it in a church or on a hilltop, it leaves an impression on the surrounding ether which never fades. The ceremony which once was performed can be celebrated again in the etheric world. All comes to life again.
>
> In the case of Stonehenge, for example, when your soul is attuned to the etheric influence of the stones, when you

---

* In the White Eagle book THE LIGHT IN BRITAIN there are many such descriptions, received by Grace Cooke when she visited a number of the sacred sites in the British Isles.

are attuned to the agelessness of life, the scales fall from your eyes and you are able to see enacted there a great and glorious heavenly scene. Is it on earth or is it in heaven? You are part of it, and the first thing you see is a vast company of angelic beings gathered there, protecting this holy light. We speak of the light buried in the stone, buried in the earth … the holy light upon the altar. Why do you think that altar is called the Rose Stone at Stonehenge? The ancient Brotherhood is still there and still enacting a grand cosmic ceremony year by year. That ceremony is as old as life itself on this earth. There are human and angelic brethren there— angels and archangels and planetary angels. We hint to you that there are glorious beings from other planets, who come to your earth because they love humanity. They come to bring light; to stimulate light in the stones on your earth. You are as the stones; these great ones come to help you: they bring indescribable spiritual power and love.

If you are fortunate enough to be able to open your vision to that scene, where there is enacted the birth of the Christ light, and to the great ceremony of the angels encircling perambulating, you will see the most beautiful movement; you will hear the tone and sound of the music of the heavens and the great paean of praise which goes forth; you will hear the very creative power and Word, which is being used as the first rays of the Sun strike the Rose Stone.

22. Archangel Michael

No book about angels would be complete without mentioning the Archangel Michael, sometimes called St Michael, who wields the sword of truth, and is at the head of all the angelic stream of life. We celebrate the Festival of St Michael and All Angels on 29th September each year, when, White Eagle says, the great archangel comes particularly close to the earth plane. He describes him thus:

> Archangel Michael is the messenger from the centre of life, one of the seven around the throne of God. A great Sun-spirit with a flashing sword, on a white horse, he heralds the coming day of the light of the spirit, which is going to break all over the earth. Archangel Michael is a being of magnificent glory and light, and it is his mission to work with all angelic beings, as a supreme leader and director of angelic life in the invisible worlds.
>
> Human minds would doubt the existence of any form of life on the sun, yet it is full of life. The form these sun spirits take is not like the human form; it is more like a circle of light. It is like the sun itself. If you can think of the human body with the head raised up and thrown back with the toes extended so that it almost forms a circle; if you can think of

forms gradually merging into the circle of light, with rays of light projecting from about the shoulder, you will perhaps get an idea of the angelic forms. We have described angels to you as bearing wings. Well, they appear to be wings: this is the best description we can give to you of these great projections of light which enable these angels to propel themselves like flashes of light through the ether.

There are many spirits of the sun, but the great messenger who visits the earth from the Sun is the one known in orthodox Christianity as the Archangel Michael. This great archangel is the head of all these life-forms on the Sun. He naturally accompanies the spirit of Christ, because Christ is the great Sun spirit, himself the spirit of the Sun, born of the Father–Mother God. And when the celebrations of the birth of Christ are made on earth, the great Archangel Michael and his attendant angels also draw near and breathe glad tidings that the Son, the prince of peace, again is born. The light of God again baptizes the earth.

Always, when there is a fresh influx of light, divine love and divine wisdom, Archangel Michael is near, and is to be seen by those who have developed sensitivity, who are gifted with vision. When the earth people prove to be more receptive to his wisdom and love, they in time will be given the vision glorious of what life might be on the earth, and what life indeed will become when the hearts of all humanity are united with the heart of the universe.

The sword which Michael wields is that of spiritual truth, which Christ places in the hand of every one of his followers—the truth of the spirit, or the Son of God indwelling within every human breast. This is the weapon which will guard you through every crisis of your human life, give you strength to overcome and put aside every obstacle. So, my children, have no fear. Attune yourselves to this invisible company of angels and you will find their power manifests in your daily life.

A trail of blazing light ... and in the light, forms ... angels ... and the Archangel Michael before us all.... He makes the sign with his sword ... the cross within the circle; and as his sword makes this sign it leaves a trail of light....

We leave you the spirit of tranquillity, of inner peace and deep thankfulness that God *is*; and that you are safe in divine love, for has not He given His angels charge over you to keep you in all your ways?

Go your way in peace; and remember that all around you are the angels of light; the angels of nature; the angels of the Christ circle.

THE WHITE EAGLE PUBLISHING TRUST is part of the wider work of the White Eagle Lodge, a place in which people may find a place for growth and understanding, and a place in which the teachings of White Eagle find practical expression. The White Eagle Lodge has many centres worldwide, but its conception is not limited to physical buildings or any one location. Here men and women may come to learn the reason for their life on earth and how to serve and live in harmony with the whole brother–sisterhood of life, visible and invisible, in health and happiness.

Readers wishing to know more of the work of the White Eagle Lodge may write to the General Secretary, The White Eagle Lodge, New Lands, Brewells Lane, Liss, Hampshire, England GU33 7HY (tel. 01730 893300) or can call at The White Eagle Lodge, 9 St Mary Abbots Place, Kensington, London W8 6LS (tel. 020-7603 7914). In the Americas please write to Church of the White Eagle Lodge, P. O. Box 930, Montgomery, Texas 77356 (tel. 409-597 5757), and in Australasia to The White Eagle Lodge (Australasia), Willomee, P. O. Box 225, Maleny, Queensland 4552 (tel. 0754 944397). A variety of activities is held at all these addresses.

You can also visit our websites at

www.whiteagle.org (UK),

www.whiteaglelodge.org (USA) and

www.whiteeaglelodge.org.au (Australasia), or e-mail us on

enquiries@whiteagle.org (UK),

enquiries@whiteaglelodge.org (USA), or

enquiries@whiteeaglelodge.org.au (Australasia).

All the White Eagle books are available by mail order from the above postal and Internet addresses but try your local bookstore first.